Intermediate 2
Woodworking Skills

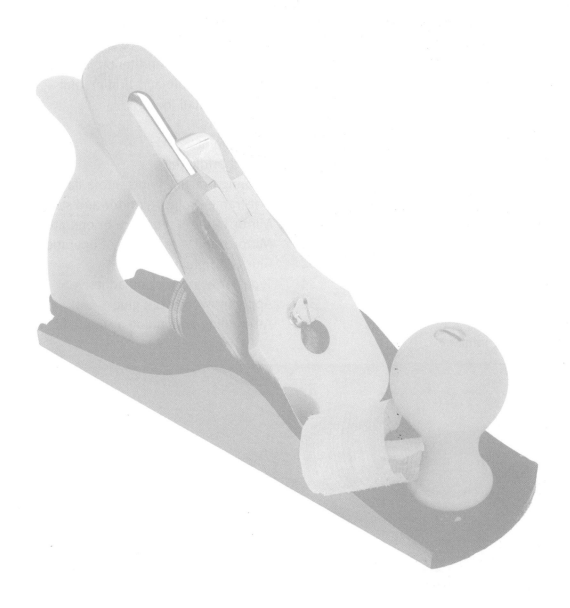

✗ John Yarr ✗

Contents

Overview

Induction

Unit 1 – Tools and Flat Frames

Contents

Unit 2 – Carcase Construction

Unit 3 – Machining and Finishing

Course Project

Index

Overview

Foreword

This guide is the result of many years' experience teaching woodwork and examining woodworking skills project work when visiting schools and colleges. If you use this book carefully, it will help you to develop practical manufacturing skills which are transferable to a number of industrial areas in the world of work.

The text follows the course stage by stage. Each project is designed so that you can learn and demonstrate a wide range of skills as the work proceeds.

Your teacher will assess you as you are working, so it is very important to work methodically and take great care with tools and machinery, being mindful of all aspects of safety. I have indicated in each chapter and at each production stage where you will have to pay greater attention to detail, because a process will be visible in the final artefact and may affect the final grade.

Remember that there is no formal exam at the end of the course. The projects you produce and the way you produce them are the things that decide what level of pass you achieve.

Finally, I would like to wish you good luck. I know that there are few things better than the joy of making something worthwhile out of wood and taking it home. You can, at the same time, learn a new craft and achieve a good grade in Woodworking Skills.

Progression

The tools, materials, joint systems and processes contained in the guide are related to success at Intermediate 2 level. They form the basis for entry to relevant further education and industry training courses, and may form part of one or more Scottish Group Awards.

Course outline

Unit/Artefact	Things you will do	Skills check
Induction	Starting points Introduction to workshop Rules of conduct Health and safety Course outline Induction material and drawings How to record your skills	Practising skills you have already learned Assessing your skills potential
Unit 1 Flat-frame Construction	Practice joints, materials and drawings Unit/artefact materials and drawings Unit test (tool recognition)	Marking out – pairing Working to tolerances Squaring and cutting shoulders Taper planning Shaping Forming joints by hand Forming joints by machine Gluing, framing and squaring Surface preparation Application of finish
Unit 2 Carcase Construction	Practice joints, materials and drawings Unit/artefact materials and drawings Two unit tests (tools, materials, processes and uses)	Marking out – pairing Working to tolerances Squaring and cutting shoulders Shaping Joint forming and fitting Surface preparation Application of finish
Unit 3 Machining and Finishing	Practice pieces (machining) Unit materials and drawings Unit test (machine tool/part identification)	Machine set-up procedures Turning to shape – tolerances Parting off to specified length Surface preparation Application of finish
Course Project	Prepare course-project materials and drawings	The range of working practices demonstrated The level of difficulty of the product The overall quality of the finished artefact The degree of independence and the amount of practical assistance required

Induction

The workshop and safety

The workbench

This figure shows a typical modern school workbench with its associated parts.

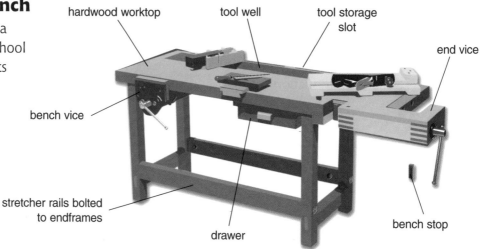

hardwood worktop   tool well   tool storage slot   end vice

bench vice

stretcher rails bolted to endframes   drawer   bench stop

The vice

The woodworking vice commonly used in school wood workshops has pieces of hardwood fixed to the inside faces of the jaws, with the top edges flush with the bench top. These act as a protection when planing, and also to provide a firm grip to the workpiece. Made of cast iron, some vices are provided with a trigger to allow the jaws to open quickly.

Bench stop

A bench stop is a small length of hardwood, square in section, that projects up through the bench top at one end. It is adjustable to various heights by means of a screw and wing-nut through a slot in the stop underneath. By placing the length of timber against the stop, and adjusting the stop height to just below the surface of the workpiece, an even shaving along the full length will produce a straight edge. It is better to use the vice for short lengths of material. (See illustration above.)

Top Tip
Although woodworking vices appear harmless, they can harm fingers if caught in the sliding bar handle, or the bar handle can catch in clothes. So, do not play with the vice.

Safety dos and don'ts

There are a number of things you should know before you start.

- Keep the vice closed when not in use to prevent anyone from colliding and causing an accident.
- Keep the surrounding floor free from loose cuttings or spills.
- Keep all tools well inside the bench so that they don't fall off and become damaged or cause accidents.
- Make sure chisels etc. do not project over the edge.
- Place steel planes on their sides on the bench when not in use.
- Keep all bags and clothing stored away from the workbench.
- Do not run in the workshop.
- All tools should be stored back in their racks and checked at the end of the work period.

Health and safety in the school workshop

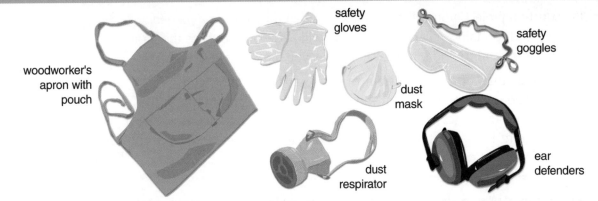

safety gloves

safety goggles

woodworker's apron with pouch

dust mask

dust respirator

ear defenders

Safety rules in the school workshop

- All woodworking machines have emergency stop buttons. These will be pointed out to you.
- When using sharp hand tools, such as chisels, always push the blade away from you, so that if you slip you will not cut yourself.
- Never wear jewellery or loose clothing. Tuck in your tie, and tie back your hair, particularly when using machine tools.
- Always wear a face chip guard or goggles when operating a wood-turning lathe.
- Wear suitable ear, nose and eye protection when appropriate.
- If, at any time when you are using a machine tool, you do not feel in complete control, always stop! If you are using a tool correctly, it should feel comfortable. So, if it does not feel comfortable, ask your teacher or instructor for guidance.
- Only one person should operate a machine tool at a time. If you are waiting to use a machine, stand outside the marked safety lines.
- In particular, when using a chisel to remove waste wood from a notch or housing joint, **always keep both hands behind the cutting edge**, and lean your left elbow (if you are right-handed) on the bench to steady yourself.
- Always store stains and polishes away when you are finished, and wipe off any spills on the workshop floor immediately.

If you use the tools the way you have been taught, and as described here, there is little chance of causing harm. However, great care should be taken at all times, especially with sharp tools, to prevent accidents to yourself or to others. Keep fingers and hands away from tools with sharp cutting edges.

Top Tip
When using sharp tools, such as chisels, keep both hands behind the cutting edge at all times.

Protect yourself from dust

All types of power sanding machines produce fine dust particles which can cause damage to your lungs if inhaled for any length of time. So, it is very important to ensure that the dust-extraction system is switched on before operating a belt or disc sander, or that a dust bag is fitted to portable machines. Eye protection must also be worn when using machines.

Quick Test

1. Name a safety measure when using the workbench.
2. Explain why.

Answers 1. Keep all sharp tools to the centre of the bench. 2. So that they don't (a) fall off and get damaged or (b) cause accidents.

Induction project – Mug tree

For the induction project, you will make either a small mug tree or a garden dibber. They both contain similar processes and will allow you to learn the basic skills for this stage and to find out what new skills you are capable of learning.

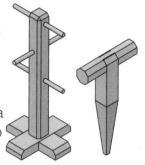

The mug tree consists of a vertical stem that is square in section and machined to size, with chamfering at the top and a small stub tenon at the bottom to fit into the base. The base consists of crossed spars incorporating a cross-halving joint in the centre and a small mortice, or socket, to take a stub mortice at the end of the stem.

Stages of manufacture

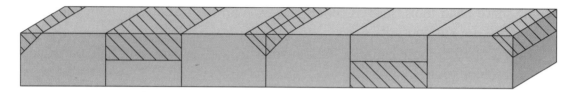

Stage 1

The cross, which is to be the base, is first squared at each end to the correct length, from one length of material for both parts, using the disc sanding machine. Then the material is marked out, taking care to transfer the sizes correctly from the working drawing. Next, using a try square, accurately transfer those sizes all round the material. The chamfers can be marked out at each end at this stage.

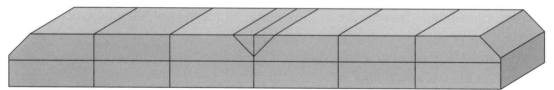

Stage 2

Set the marking gauge to the depth of the notches (half the thickness), and gauge on the depth between the appropriate marked lines.

Using the tenon saw and sawing board, saw down to the gauge-line, just to the waste side of the notch lines, taking great care not to saw below the gauge-lines.

With the material held in the vice, remove the waste from both notches in the four stages A, B, C and D shown, using a bevel-edged chisel, keeping the bevelled side upwards and resting your elbow on the bench for balance.

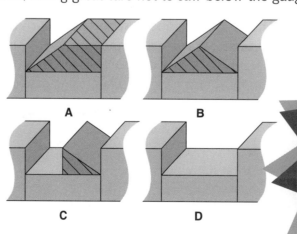

A   B   C   D

Top Tip
Ensure that you mark out the waste wood to be removed and that one notch is at the top and one at the bottom. Do not halve the material until the very end.

Stages of manufacture (cont.)

Form chamfers at each end by vertical chiselling using the bevel-edged chisel with a board underneath and finishing off on the disc sanding machine.

Stage 3 CUT

Saw down the centre line parting the two pieces, which can then be paired.

Fit, glue and clamp the cross-halving joint using a G clamp, ensuring that it is all square and true (not warped).

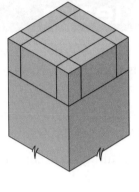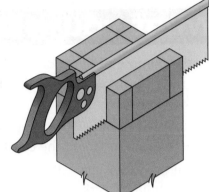

The stem

Square the ends of the stem to the correct length on the disc sanding machine.

Mark and drill out the position of the pegs for hanging mugs.

Form a small stub tenon at the bottom of the stem as follows: Set the marking gauge to around 4 mm and lightly gauge on the end from each face; measure the length of the stub tenon from the end and square mark all round; mark out the waste round the outside of the stub tenon; and, holding the work in the vice, saw down carefully to the waste side of the gauge-lines as shown.

Carefully saw down the shoulders on all four sides.

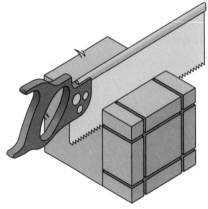

The stub mortice

Form the mortice in the centre of the crossed base by drawing diagonals to find the centre. Using the correct size of Forstner bit in the pillar drill, bore down to the pre-set depth.

Square off the sides of the mortice carefully by vertical chiselling.

Finish off the base and stem with sandpaper, removing all blemishes and pencil marks. Fit, glue and clamp the stem into the base. Cut the dowels to length, round the ends with a cabinet file, and sandpaper. Lightly tap the pegs into the prepared holes using a small amount of glue, and clean off surplus glue.

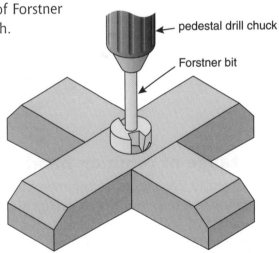

pedestal drill chuck

Forstner bit

Quick Test

1. Why is it important to saw just to the waste side of the line when sawing down the sides of a notch in a cross-halving joint?

2. When cutting out a notch using a chisel, what method of control would be used?

Answers 1 So that the joint will fit tightly. 2. Hold the chisel handle with one hand and the blade over-grasp with the other.

Unit 1 – Tools and Flat Frames

What you will learn

For the purpose of this course, a flat frame is defined as a timber frame whose four sides consist of material that is lying flat, such as a door, picture frame, window frame etc.

This unit has been designed to incorporate a wide range of woodworking processes appropriate to the construction of flat frames.

The unit provides you with the opportunity to accumulate knowledge, understanding and skills in fundamental areas of practical woodworking. You will be encouraged to be independent and to make appropriate choices in the use of tools and materials and to learn the importance of safety and of responsible conduct in a workshop environment. You will be assessed on personal development with regard to practical capability.

You will produce a range of finished joints that should be retained for assessment and external sampling. The purpose of the unit is the manufacture of a flat-frame project. Generally, the best joint should be considered for assessment.

While the unit may be taught in sequence, the project should be considered at an early stage, and you will be encouraged to practise those joints and the use of materials and processes that will be appropriate to its manufacture.

Example of project

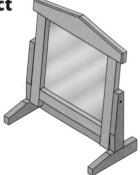

Use a range of common hand tools

You will learn to use a range of common hand tools. This will include learning their component parts; setting and sharpening; and the care, maintenance and proper use of a range of joinery bench tools such as planes, chisels, marking-out tools, basic jigs, cramps and mitre boxes.

The range of tools and equipment contained in this guide is appropriate for Intermediate 2 level. You will learn and be tested on:

- tool recognition and identifying their parts;
- the proper use, handling and storage of tools;
- the selection of an appropriate tool for each process;
- checking for faults and how to correct these faults;
- observing all current health and safety regulations with regard to school workshop practice and safety legislation.

Top Tip
Try to plan each stage of the work so that there are as few tools as possible on the bench.

Make a range of woodworking joints

You will make a range of woodworking joints. This will include the identification and preparation of materials, and setting out and making a range of basic joints that can be used in a wide range of flat-frame joinery fabrications and structures. These joints will include the butt joint, corner halving, cross-halving, tee-halving, mortice and tenon, dowelled, and dovetail joints.

The range of woodworking joints contained in this guide is appropriate for Intermediate 2 level and slightly beyond in some processes. You will learn and be tested on:

- planing sawn and machined wood to within specified sizes;
- marking out and 'drawing in' woodworking joints to within specified sizes;
- fitting and finishing woodworking joints to within specified sizes;
- observing all current health and safety regulations with regard to school workshop practice.

Manufacture a product from a working drawing

You will manufacture a framed product from a working drawing.

This will include the teaching and learning of the use, application and possible modification of working drawings, the practical use of cutting lists, setting out using rods and templates, drawing in, and the selection and use of appropriate joints and frame assembly, including squaring and cramping.

The range of woodworking processes contained in this guide is appropriate for Intermediate 2 level. You will learn and be tested on:

- checking and confirming that the material provided is correct in both quantity and size;
- setting out the product within specified tolerances;
- manufacturing the product to within specified tolerances;
- observing all current health and safety regulations with regard to school workshop practice and safety legislation.

Quick Test

1. The course consists of three units: flat-frame, carcase and machining. Why does the course project contain these same three elements?

Answer 1. To give you a second chance to perfect the skills learned in the units.

Common hand tools and their use

Measuring and marking-out tools

If you are to produce straight and square lengths of wood to within tolerances in the construction of flat frames, carcases and machined products, it is essential that the measuring and marking-out tools are kept as accurate as possible. All marking-out tools should be handled with great care at all times.

The steel rule

The steel rule is now commonly used in school workshops. These are provided in a 300 mm size for bench use and 1 metre lengths for taking larger sizes. The main advantage of the steel rule is that the graduations start from the end, and measuring is more accurate than measuring tapes and wooden rules. The steel rule can also be used for checking surfaces and edges for trueness and can also be bent slightly to scribe curves.

The try square

All lines across the wood surface should be marked along the blade of the try square with the handle held tight against the face or edge of the material.

Checking the accuracy of a try square

Because try squares are in constant use, it is best to check their accuracy from time to time. Draw a line at right angles to the edge of the workpiece. Turn the square over and slide the blade up to the marked line. The square will line up perfectly with the marked line if it is accurate.

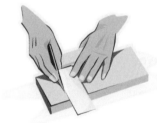

Squaring a mark across and all round the timber

Place the point of the pencil or marking knife on the mark.

Holding the handle towards you with the brass face tight against the timber, and the blade flat down on the surface, move the blade along until it rests against the pencil or knife, and draw across. This action can be repeated until the line is squared all round the timber.

Sliding bevel

A sliding bevel is a 'try square' which can be set at any angle, or bevel, by means of a locking screw or lever. The handle can also be slid along the slot in the blade and locked in any position for working in corners.

Top Tip
When squaring across the shoulders of a number of rails of the same length, it is better to clamp them together and square them across all together, then separate them and square round all sides of each rail. Make sure the lines meet exactly at the corners.

Setting a sliding bevel

Slacken the locking lever just enough for the blade to move; set the required angle against a protractor or known angle, then retighten the lever.

The marking gauge

The marking gauge is used for marking the correct width and thickness on a length of wood. It is normally made of beech and consists of four parts The **stock**, or fence, slides along the **stem** and is held in place by means of a **thumbscrew**. The parallel line is scribed by means of a steel **marking pin** set into the end of the stem.

Setting a marking gauge

Set the rule against the stock with the thumbscrew just slackened, and the rule behind the pin as shown. You should be able to move the stock with one hand until the **marking** pin is at the exact distance. Tighten the thumbscrew and check the setting. If necessary, make fine adjustments by tapping either end of the stem against the bench as shown.

Using a marking gauge

Place the stem on the workpiece with the pin pointing towards you, then slide the stock up against the side of the work. Slide the gauge up and down two or three times until you feel a comfortable grip. Rotate the tool until the pin begins to mark the wood, then push the gauge away from you to scribe a clear and straight line.

The mortice gauge

The mortice gauge is used for marking out the two sides of a mortice and therefore is fitted with two marking pins on the end of the stem. The distance between the pins is controlled by means of a screw set into the end of the stem and is locked in place by a brass screw. Most mortice gauges have a single marking pin set into the reverse side of the stem and can be used also as a marking gauge.

Setting a mortice gauge

The distance between the pins is adjusted by means of the end screw to the width of the mortice chisel to be used. Before locking the stock, set the two pins roughly in the centre of the material thickness, and gauge lightly from each side until the pins are exactly in the centre. The same gauge setting must be used to mark out the matching tenons.

Top Tip
When marking on mortices and tenons, always gauge from the identified face side of each member.

Quick Test

1. Why are steel rules more accurate when working on small components?

2. What is the essential difference between a marking gauge and a mortice gauge? Explain the use of each tool.

Answers 1. The steel rule is more accurate for small sizes because the graduations start right at the end. **2** A marking gauge has only one marking pin for scribing lines parallel to a straight edge, whereas a mortice gauge has two marking pins for scribing the two parallel sides of a mortice-and-tenon joint.

Planes and planing

The bench planes used in most school workshops are now made of cast steel and can be divided into two categories: **general-purpose** planes, and **special** planes used for specific purposes.

General-purpose bench planes

Jack plane

The 350 mm jack plane is used mostly for planing material down to size (for example, planing down to a **gauge line**) and is the main tool for preparing the material referred to in this guide. When setting up a workpiece against the **bench stop** for planing, the grain should be rising up towards the front. However, the material should be reversed if the first shaving is rough.

All metal bench planes are made with similar parts and are dismantled in the same way. The blade and cap-iron are held in place by means of a **lever cap**, and the depth of cut is adjusted by means of a screw.

> **Top Tip**
> It is often easier to smooth irregular grain if you use a slicing action by turning the plane at a slight angle to the direction of travel.

To ensure you have control over the direction of the plane, the handle is held firmly with the forefinger pointing forwards and the other hand holding down the toe by means of the round knob at the front. To ensure a smooth action and good balance, both feet are placed apart, with pressure on the toe of the plane at the start of the stroke and on the handle at the end to avoid any rounding off. During the planing operation, look down and check that there is a straight line from your shoulder through your arm to the toe of the plane.

> **Top Tip**
> The block plane is a good plane for cutting end grain.

Smoothing plane

At 225 mm long, the smoothing plane is the smallest of the general-purpose planes in use today and is ideal for final shaping and finishing work.

Rebate plane

This essential tool has an adjustable **fence** and a **depth stop**, with the blade mounted near the toe. It is used mainly for forming edge rebates.

Block plane

The block plane is used single-handedly for shaping and trimming.

Shoulder plane

With its cutting iron set at a low angle, the metal shoulder plane is ideal for trimming the end grain on shoulders of broad carcase joints.

Bull-nose plane

A minature version of the shoulder plane, the bull-nose plane is useful for trimming small joints.

Special-purpose bench planes

Router plane

The router plane, or Granny's Tooth, is designed for smoothing the bottom of the cross-grain grooves in housing joints. The depth is adjusted by lowering or raising the cutter and tightening with a thumbscrew.

Plough plane

Used for forming grooves parallel to an edge, the plough plane can be adjusted both in depth of cut and distance from the edge by means of a depth stop and side fence. The tool is usually supplied with a set of interchangeable cutters ranging from 3 mm to 12 mm wide.

Combination plane

This is a more sophisticated plane than the plough plane and can be used to cut an even wider groove or to form a raised **moulding** along a finished edge.

Quick Test

1. What is the difference between general-purpose and special-purpose planes?
2. What do all metal bench planes have in common?
3. What is the smallest general-purpose plane in use today? How long is it?
4. What would a plough plane be used for?

Answers 1. General-purpose planes can be used for everyday planing while special-purpose planes have specific uses. **2.** All metal bench planes are made with similar parts and are dismantled in the same way. **3** The smoothing plane is the smallest and measures only 225 mm in length. **4** The plough plane is used for cutting narrow grooves parallel to the edge, and can be used with a range of interchangeable cutters, from 3 mm to 12 mm wide.

Chisels and their use

There are three basic types of chisel. These are firmer chisels, bevel-edged or paring chisels, and mortice chisels. Each is designed to perform distinctly different tasks.

Firmer chisels

Firmer chisels, as the name suggests, have a stout blade of rectangular section and are used mainly for the heavier work of cutting out deeper joints. Wooden handles have largely been replaced by polypropylene moulded into the shank of the chisel.

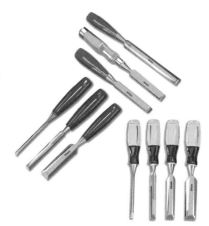

Bevel-edged chisels

These are more slender than firmer chisels, having the edges of the blade tapered off, allowing the chisel to be worked into corners. This is especially useful for cleaning up joints. Like most chisels produced nowadays, bevel-edged chisels are fitted with a moulded polypropylene handle to withstand light tapping with a mallet. With a well-sharpened chisel, bodyweight is normally sufficient to cut through wood cleanly.

Mortice chisels

These are much stronger than other types of chisels, having a thicker blade that is long and tapered so that it can be used to lever out waste during the cutting of deep mortices.

Vertical paring

This process is used for removing a small corner or when fitting a joint. The chisel is held vertically, using your bodyweight above.

It is essential to place a piece of scrap wood under the workpiece and fasten it firmly to the bench by means of a G clamp.

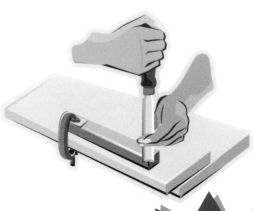

Hold the bevel-edged chisel vertically between the thumb and forefinger of the left hand, with the thumb behind and the bevelled side outward. The back of the chisel should rest against your middle finger to provide control, with your left hand resting on the workpiece.

With the chisel held over the part to be pared off, and your right shoulder over the chisel handle to provide weight, hold the chisel firmly in your right hand and slice downwards, moving the chisel gently from side to side in a controlled action. It is important not to try to pare too much off at each cut.

Top Tip
Place the left elbow comfortably on the bench to steady and help control the process.

Horizontal paring

Put the joint to be cleaned up into the vice just above the marking gauge line to which you are working.

Let the chisel blade rest (bevel edge up) across all four fingers of your left hand (palm uppermost). Your left hand gives the control. Hold the chisel in place with your thumb about halfway down.

Either push the chisel into the wood using the pad of your right hand against the handle (perhaps lightly tapping the chisel with the fleshy part of your hand), or firmly grip the handle with your right hand and push towards the wood. The aim is to gently push or strike the chisel handle, carefully cutting into the wood.

> **Top Tip**
> For extra control, it may be better to hold the blade of the chisel overgrasp with your left hand and rest the same elbow on the bench.

The mortice chisel and its use

Always secure the workpiece firmly either in the vice or clamped to the bench on top of a chopping or sawing board, or on a piece of scrap wood as shown.

Hold the chisel vertically with your left hand; or you can hold the blade for greater control.

Carefully position the chisel between the mortice gauge marks about 2 mm from the end of the mortice with the bevel away from you. Give the handle of the chisel a light tap with the side of the mallet. Move the chisel blade outwards and repeat, delivering only light taps to form a series of cuts along the length of the mortice.

> **Top Tip**
> Keep both hands behind the cutting edge at all times.

Stop about 2 mm from the other end – this is to protect against showing spaces outside the line – and, with the forefinger under the blade, carefully lever out the chippings from this first layer. Repeat this operation, keeping the chisel vertical at all times and only tapping lightly each time until you reach halfway. Then reverse the workpiece and repeat the process for a through mortice. (See pp. 39–41, 'Flat-frame joints': through and haunched mortice-and-tenon joints.)

Quick Test

1. Explain the shape and use of bevel-edged and firmer chisels.

2. Why is it important when using a mortice chisel to hold the tool vertically?

3. Why is it important when using a mortice chisel to stop just before the end line of the mortice?

Answers **1.** A bevel-edged chisel is so shaped to get into corners when paring; and a firmer chisel is so shaped, as the name suggests, to be stronger for levering out waste wood, as with mortice chisels. **2.** So that the mortice will be true and the resulting joint will not be twisted. **3.** So that, when levering out the waste chippings from the mortice, you don't cut past the line and show a gap in the finished joint.

Caring for planes and chisels

Adjusting and sharpening

The most common cause of poorly formed joints, rough edges and surfaces is blunt-edged tools. The best plane or chisel in the world is useless without a sharp cutting edge. The best way to improve the quality of your work is to recognise when a chisel is blunt and when a plane iron is either blunt or **maladjusted**, or both.

The sharpening stone

Most modern sharpening stones are made of graded **synthetic** material, and come in medium and fine grades for light workshop use. The edge is first sharpened on the medium side and finished off on the fine surface to obtain a good edge. When sharpening edges, it is essential to lubricate the stone with light engineering oil, otherwise the friction will cause the steel to heat up and the edge to be rough. To even out the wear on an oilstone, care must be taken to run the blade over the whole area. A figure-of-eight pattern is a good habit to develop, as shown.

Sharpening a plane blade (plane iron)

This process should initially be done under close supervision. The back of a plane iron should be absolutely flat so that, when the cap-iron is fitted to the edge (leaving around 2 mm), there should be no gap between to allow shavings to push through and clog the plane instead of being deflected up out of the plane mouth. The first stage of sharpening a plane blade, therefore, is to flatten the back on the sharpening stone or hone, as shown. This is called backing off.

The plane blade, like most edge-cutting tools, is ground on a grinding wheel to an angle of about 25 degrees. The cutting edge is formed by honing, or sharpening, on a Carborundum stone to approximately 30 degrees. These angles are approximate but need only be not too steep or shallow. When you start honing, you should try to lock your wrist so that the angle remains constant and not rounded. As you hone the sharpening angle, a burr is formed at the back of the blade. The edge is finally sharpened by **backing off** the blade to remove this burr. The action of sharpening and backing off is repeated until a keen edge is formed, which can be checked by your teacher.

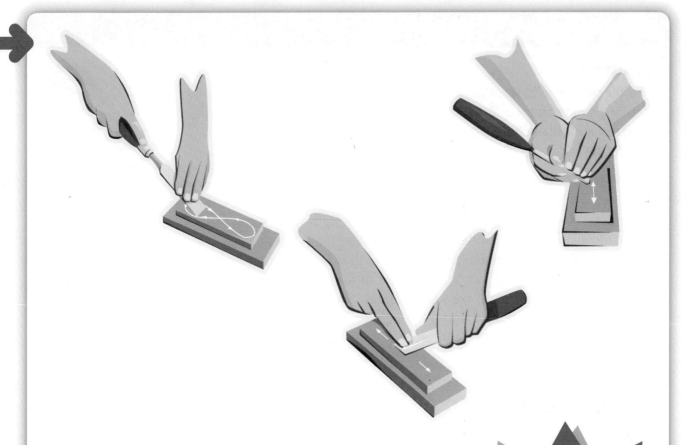

Sharpening chisels

Chisels are sharpened in exactly the same way as plane irons. As with most other wood-cutting blades, the flat side at the back must be perfectly flat and the bevelled side ground to the correct angle. Both chisels and plane iron should be checked regularly for sharpness by use (not by trying the blade with a finger), and also for dents in the cutting edge. Any of these defects should be reported to the teacher, as they will affect the quality of your work. Care should be taken when sharpening narrow chisels and to spread the wear over the entire surface of the sharpening stone.

Top Tip
When rubbing the back of a cutting-edged tool on the sharpening stone, you can ensure it is absolutely flat by checking for brightness caused by rubbing. This brightness should extend along the back of the cutting edge.

Storage and handling of chisels

Chisels and all tools with sharp cutting edges should be stored in a rack where the sharp edges are protected from damage and so that there is no danger of accidental cuts when selecting for use. Great care should be taken when carrying a chisel in the workshop. The cutting edge should be placed between the thumb and forefinger and carried with the handle tucked inside the arm so that there is no danger to others when passing.

Quick Test

1. What is the main cause of a plane becoming clogged up with shavings?

2. When using a sharpening stone, or oilstone, why is it necessary to back up?

Answers 1. The cap-iron or cover is fitted too close to the cutting edge, and to rub off any burrs on the 2. So that the flat side of the plane iron remains truly flat.

Saws and their use

Handsaws

Used for cutting solid wood and man-made boards into smaller sizes for planing and use in flat-frame and carcase construction, handsaws are usually hollow-ground – they taper from the line of teeth to the back edge to allow clearance in the saw-cut or kerf.

Crosscut saw

With teeth specially designed for cutting across the wood-grain fibres, the crosscut saw is ideally suited to cutting timber to length. Each tooth leans backwards at an angle of 14 degrees. This is called the pitch and may vary slightly according to the manufacture. Each tooth is filed sharp at its tip and is bent sideways in each direction alternately to form the cut or kerf. This is called the set of the saw. If the saw becomes jammed in the kerf, it is usually due to the set being reduced through use. Crosscut saw blades are generally about 600 mm long, with seven to eight points per 25 mm.

Panel saw

This is essentially a smaller version of the crosscut saw. Having 10 points per 25 mm, it is used mainly for cutting man-made boards.

Tenon saws

These are referred to as back saws and are the most commonly used saws in school workshops. They have a blade strengthened with either a brass or a steel strip. This helps to keep the blade rigid for cutting accurate mortice-and-tenon joints. The blade length is 250–350 mm and usually has 13–15 points per 25 mm.

Dovetail saw

A fine back saw designed to cut accurate joints such as the dovetail joint. The blade length is 200 mm, and there are 16–22 points per 25 mm.

Using a tenon or back saw

This procedure is generally the same for all saws. With the saw held in the right hand with the forefinger pointing forwards to give control and direction, start by drawing the saw towards you from the far side of the material. Place the thumb of your other hand against the blade just above the teeth as a guide until the cut is started. Now lightly push the saw away from you without holding the handle too tightly or letting the saw bounce. The important thing is to relax while sawing and not to try to force the action, or else the saw will jam in the kerf.

Top Tip
While you are sawing, from your elbow through your wrist to the point of the saw should be a straight line – looking down.

Coping saw

A coping saw has a metal frame, and the blade is anchored at either end in a **slotted retaining pin**. The handle is attached to one retaining pin, and the blade can be tightened or slackened by turning the handle while holding the retaining pin.

Controlling the coping saw

To prevent the blade from wandering off line while cutting, place your extended forefinger on the frame of the coping saw. If this feels comfortable, close the other hand around the first to form a double-handed grip.

Top Tip
Always use the saw with a smooth motion. Do not jerk, and always keep the pins aligned.

Making closed cuts

When cutting a hole with the coping saw, mark out the work and bore a small access hole for the blade just inside the curve. Slacken off the blade, pass it through the hole and reconnect to the frame.

Replacing a damaged coping-saw blade

While holding the pin attached to the handle end of the frame, turn the handle anticlockwise to loosen the blade fixing. Attach the blade to the opposite end from the handle with teeth pointing away from the handle, and, leaning the frame against the bench to reduce the distance between the retaining pins, fit the blade to the handle end of the frame and tighten the handle while holding the pin as before. Make sure the pins on the frame are lined up, or the blade will be twisted.

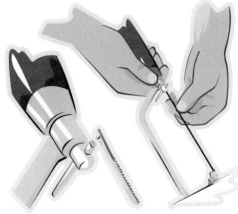

Quick Test

1. Explain the meaning of a 'saw kerf'.

2. What is the purpose of the metal strip on the back of a tenon saw?

3. Why do the teeth of all crosscut saws point forwards?

Answers 1. A saw kerf is the cut made by the saw when cutting through wood. The splay of alternate teeth determines its width. **2** To stiffen the blade for long, straight cuts. **3** Because all crosscut saws only cut on the forward stroke, while the kerf is cleared on the back stroke.

Hand drilling and boring tools

Hand drill or wheel brace

Due to the increased use of portable power drills, the hand drill is now used less frequently. However, it is still a very useful tool to have in the school workshop, requiring only muscle energy to crank the handle. The spring-loaded chuck is designed to take a wide range of twist drills.

Twist drills

Twist drills, as the name suggests, have two spiral flutes or channels that clear the cuttings from the hole during the drilling process. The point of the drill bit has two cutting edges at the ends of the flutes, and versions can now cut metal as well as wood. Hand drills are capable of taking drills up to 9 mm diameter.

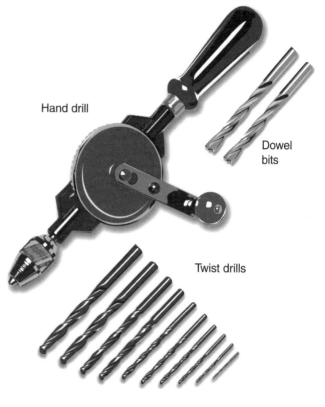

Hand drill

Dowel bits

Twist drills

Ratchet brace

The ratchet brace consists of a frame, a cranking handle, a chuck at one end and a round handle at the top. The frame is cranked in a clockwise direction as the handle at the top is pressed down. The circle of the cranking handle is known as the sweep, and 250 mm is the standard size used in school workshops.

In order to operate the brace in confined spaces, the chuck is fitted with a ratchet to allow a partial sweep and reverse motion. The forward, reverse and lock action is operated by means of a cam ring behind the chuck.

Auger bits

Auger bits for a ratchet brace come in sizes up to 25 mm with a helical twist-ending in cutting edges for removing wood waste. Two very important features of the auger bit are the sharp twin spurs for cutting a clean circular hole and the central worm screw for pulling the bit into the wood.

Fitting a bit into a ratchet brace

Lock the brace ratchet by centring the **cam ring**, then grip the chuck in one hand and turn the frame clockwise. Drop a bit into the chuck and reverse the process to close the jaws.

Top Tip
When boring a hole with a wheel brace or ratchet brace, always pull the tool out of the hole while it is still turning – this gives a clean finish.

Boring with a brace

With the brace held vertically in one hand, place the point of the auger lead screw exactly on the marked hole centre, and crank the handle with the other. The same procedure is adopted when boring a hole horizontally with the workpiece held in the vice. In both cases, a scrap piece of wood should be clamped behind the hole to avoid ragged edges; and it is helpful to have someone standing to the side to check the brace alignment.

Countersink bits

Countersink bits are used to form a tapered recess at the top of a drilled hole to take the head of a wood screw so that it lies flush with the wood surface. Always start gently and try the upturned screw head into the sinking to determine the number of turns required.

Screwdriver bits

This special bit converts the ratchet brace into a heavy-duty screwdriver.

Bradawls

Modern versions of this simple tool consist of a length of wire forged and flattened at one end and moulded into a polypropylene handle. Insert the tool across the grain, and bore using hand pressure to cut the wood fibres. This forms a starter hole for the wood screw. Traditional types have a wooden handle.

Expansive bits

Expansive bits are designed with a movable cutter which is adjustable to bore holes up to 75 mm in diameter, depending on the model type.

Centre bits

Since centre bits are designed to bore relatively shallow holes, from 12 mm to 68 mm deep, they are simpler and therefore cheaper than the equivalent auger bits.

Quick Test

1. What is the purpose of the spurs on the end of an auger bit?
2. What is the purpose of a bradawl?

Answers 1. The spurs on the end of an auger bit project down and form a circular part for the main boring cutters. Without these spurs, a very ragged hole would be produced. 2. A bradawl is used to bore a starting hole for screws, especially in hardwood, to prevent splitting.

Hammers, mallets and screwdrivers

Claw hammer

This is the standard joinery tool for driving and extracting nails. The claw hammer is produced in different weights to suit a range of driving situations ranging from light bench work to constructing with heavy sawn softwood. The head of the claw hammer is case-hardened, which means that it is hard on the outside and soft in the centre to drive even toughened masonry nails. Modern versions are steel-shafted with a moulded rubber or plastic grip.

Cross peen hammer

Sometimes spelt cross pein, this is the hammer most used for light pin-driving and joint-assembly work in school workshops. The peen is used for starting small panel pins and nails, and the wooden handle is shaped for a comfortable grip.

Wooden mallet

This tool is specially designed for situations where damage could be caused by the use of a metal hammer, such as hand morticing, assembling, dismantling frames and carcases striking wood on wood. The tapered shaft is morticed into the head so that it remains fixed and so that the tapered beechwood head will strike a chisel fairly each time.

Top Tip
Always hold a hammer near the end of the shaft to obtain a good balance for striking, never hold it near the head.

Top Tip
When chopping out mortices, use a controlled clean stroke. To maintain good control a number of short gentle taps is better. And you might find more comfort when using the side of the mallet head – evenly and squarely.

Nail punch

This is a punch made of **tool steel**, and it is used to drive nail and pin heads below the wood surface. It is tapered with a serrated grip and is hollow at the tip to prevent the punch from slipping off the nail head.

Top Tip
When driving the nail, use the little finger of your left hand to guide the punch on to the nail head before striking.

Screwdrivers

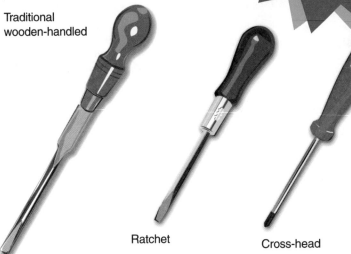

Traditional wooden-handled

Ratchet

Cross-head

Cabinet screwdrivers

The traditional slot screwdriver is fitted with a wooden or plastic handle, and comes in different sizes with a flat taper-ground tip to fit a range of screws.

Cross-head screwdriver

This tool has become very popular for use with modern advanced cross-head fast-action and double-helical screw nails. The cross-head is designed with four **flutes** to form a more positive grip between screwdriver and screw.

Ratchet screwdrivers

Provided with a forward, reverse and lock ratchet mechanism so that the hand stays on the handle in operation, portable power screwdrivers have largely replaced these once very useful tools.

Quick Test

1. Why is it better to use a hammer by holding the shaft near the end?

2. Describe the use of a nail punch.

3. Why is it important to use a screwdriver with a point that fits the screw head?

Answers 1. To obtain a better balance and more striking power. 2. A nail punch is used with a hammer to drive nail and pin heads beneath the wood surface. 3 So that the screwdriver does not slip off the screw slot and spoil the work. A cross-head that is too big will also spoil the screw.

Clamps and benchvice

G clamp

Sometimes referred to as a G cramp, this is an excellent general-purpose clamp that is often used to hold a workpiece to the bench while you work on it. Usually made from cast iron, the frame forms a fixed jaw. The clamping force is applied by a screw fitted with a ball-jointed shoe. G clamps are manufactured in a range of sizes.

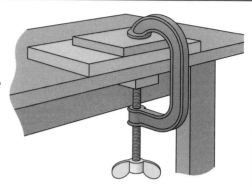

Always protect the workpiece and the workbench with a protective block.

Woodwork bench vice

One of the most important general-purpose holding tools in the school workshop (see p. 6)

Sash clamps

These are supplied in various lengths to suit a range of frame and carcase clamping situations. They consist of a long steel bar with a screw-adjustable jaw at one end and another bar that slides along the bar and can be located in various positions by a steel pin fitted through holes in the bar.

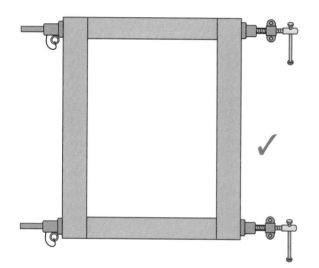

sash clamp and frame being glued

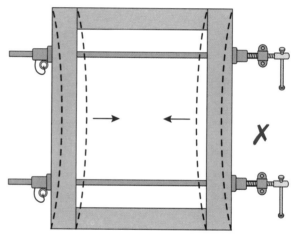

Position clamp to align with centre of joint – if not, the frame will distort as more pressure is applied.

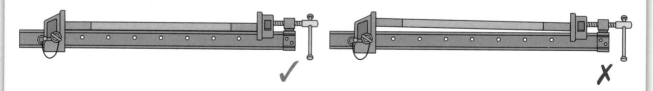

Keep frame flat on sash clamps, or use packing pieces of even thickness underneath – even a slight gap will cause problems.

Fast screw clamps

Fast screw clamps are designed for speedy adjustment to fit the size of the work. Various sizes and lengths are in use, and the sash type has a pistol grip with a quick-release button.

Clamping a frame

When gluing up an assembly, it pays to prepare the work area in advance in order to avoid delays in the process. Place battens of the same thickness across the bench to rest the frame on when clamping. It is always better to do this job with a helper at the other side of the bench to handle the clamps.

Clamping a frame

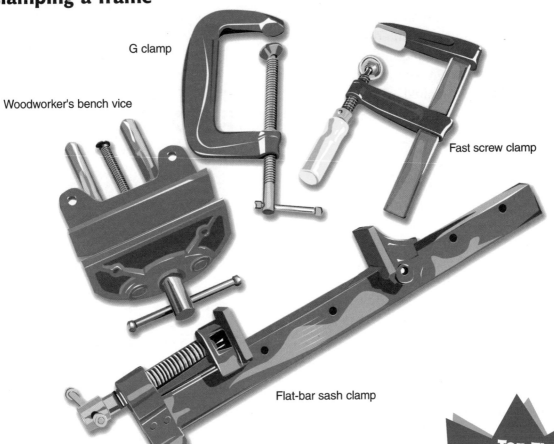

Woodworker's bench vice

G clamp

Fast screw clamp

Flat-bar sash clamp

Checking a frame for square

With a steel measuring tape or thin wooden rod pointed at the end, check the size of the diagonals inside the frame. If the frame is exactly square, these two sizes should be the same. If the diagonals are different, you can slacken off the clamps slightly and set them at a slight angle to pull the frame square. Then check the diagonals again. (See p. 59, 'Checking for square'.)

Top Tip
Make sure you take extra care when clamping up. Always ensure the clamps are in the correct position. The glue dries fairly quickly, and you will only have one chance to get it right.

Quick Test

1. Explain the term 'dry framing'.
2. Describe a method of testing a frame for square.

Answers 1. Dry framing is used to clamp a frame together without glue to ensure that all the joints are tight-fitting and square.
2 Measure and compare the size of the frame diagonals, or use a try square to test the inside of the frame.

Jigs and fixings

Making a depth jig

This easily constructed jig is useful in situations where you want a number of dowels to project out the same distance. If the dowels are to project out 15 mm, drill a hole slightly larger than the dowel in a piece of wood 15 mm thick. By entering each dowel into its hole, and placing the jig over the dowel, as shown, you can tap the dowels down to the required 15 mm projection. (See p.33, 'Dowelled joints').

Making a stop block

Making a simple stop block is the simplest way to ensure that a number of holes are drilled to exactly the same depth. First, fit the appropriate drill into the chuck of the wheel brace or power drill. If you want to drill holes exactly say 15 mm deep, cut a piece of block to the length of drill projecting from the chuck minus 15 mm. Drill through the block to the full depth of the drill, and the jig is complete.

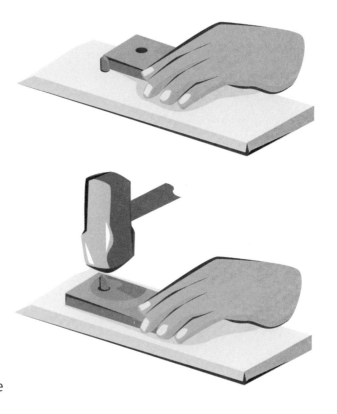

Using a stop collar

A collar fixed to the shank of a drill bit at the required position can also be used to drill holes of uniform depth. This tool can be fixed to the drill bit with an Allen key for use with power drills or a wheel brace.

Bolt and barrel nut fixing

This is a common fixing used in a wide range of flat-packed DIY leg-and-frame rail assemblies. The fixing consists of a bolt threaded through a steel barrel at right angles. The barrel is fitted into a pre-drilled hole in the rail and lined up with the bolt by a screw-driver in a slot. The bolt is inserted through a pre-drilled hole in the leg and the rail end to meet the barrel and tightened securely.

Top Tip
Some stop collars are formed as countersink bits for drilling screw holes and countersinking at the same time.

Block joints

This simple surface-mounted fixing consists of interlocking plastic blocks screwed on the inside of carcase cabinet corners or to fix shelves. Moulded dowels on one half of the joint locate with sockets in the other.

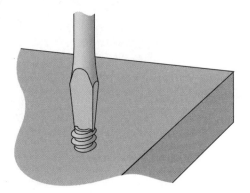 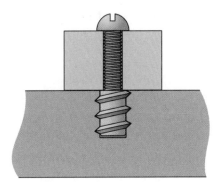

Fitting the socket blocks

Mark the thickness of the board on the inside of the carcase side panel. Mark the position of two block joints about 50 mm from the front and back edges. Align the base of each socket block with the marked lines, and screw it to the panel.

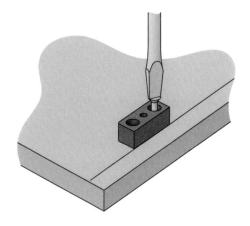 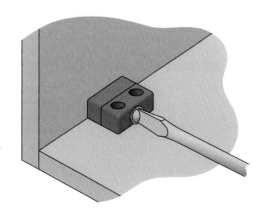

Fitting the dowel blocks

Holding the panels together at right angles, fit the mating dowel blocks and mark their fixing holes on the other board. Screw the blocks in place, and assemble with the clamping bolts.

Quick Test

1. What is the main purpose of block joints and dowel blocks, and what is their advantage?

Answer 1. So that parts can be assembled and disassembled easily and quickly.

Common nails and wood screws

Nails and pins and their use

- Round wire nail – a strong nail made from a round steel wire with a flat head fitted with **serrations** so that the hammer does not slip. Used for general joinery and construction work.

- Oval wire or oval brad – general-purpose nail made from oval-section steel wire. Designed to reduce the chance of the wood splitting.

- Lost-head nail – a round-section nail with a small head that allows it to be punched below the surface of the wood.

- Panel pin – used to fasten thin plywood, hardboard or Medium Density Fibreboard (MDF), or to secure small joints or mouldings. Deep-drive panel pins have a conical head to reduce the need for sinking the head.

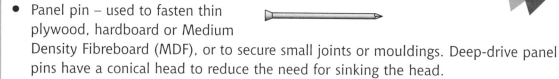

Top Tip

Insert nails into a joint at alternating angles so the nails grip the grain. This is called dovetail nailing and produces a stronger joint than straight nailing.

Wood screws

These are used to fix two or more pieces of material together. There are a number of factors that will determine what wood screw to use for a particular situation: the thread of the screw, the type of screw, the type of head, the materials to be joined and their thickness.

Materials wood screws are made of

- Steel is the most common but will rust if used for external work if not protected. Not to be used in oak, as they will tarnish because of the **tannic acid** produced.

- Since brass screws are non-ferrous, they will not rust and are very decorative. Care should be taken when driving brass screws, as they are brittle and may break easily.

- Black japanned or black enamelled screws are used mainly for fittings on exterior doors and gates.

- Chromium-plated, electro-brassed, nickel-plated or stainless steel wood screws are used for a number of special fixing situations.

Screw heads and threads

- Raised head. Generally used to fasten handles and fittings to wood cabinets.

- Countersunk. This is the most common screw head. The clearance hole will need to be countersunk (using a countersink bit) to allow the top of the screw to sit flush, or slightly below the wood surface.

- Round head. The shoulder of the screw lies flush with the surface of the fitting. Mostly used for fitting ironmongery or furniture ironmongery.

- Slotted head. This is the traditional simple slot across the head, into which the screwdriver fits.

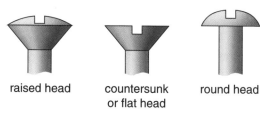

raised head   countersunk or flat head   round head

slotted head   crosspoint head

- Crosspoint head. Designed to prevent the screwdriver slipping and damaging the work. Crosspoint screws will not withstand the same amount of leverage as slotted types, so it is very important to use a screwdriver point that fits exactly into the screw head.
- Traditional wood screw. Used to fasten softwoods, hardwoods, MDF and plywoods in cabinet work and general woodwork.
- Twin thread. Very keen pulling power. The twin thread is especially suitable for fastening man-made sheet materials, as its grip is much stronger than traditional wood screws.

traditional wood screw

twin thread wood screw

Driving in a wood screw

To drive in a wood screw and join two pieces of wood successfully, the following points must be considered.

- Determine the number of screws to be used, and mark their positions.
- Consider the thicknesses of the two pieces of wood and determine the appropriate screw length, so that the screw does not penetrate right through.
- Determine the core, or root diameter, of the screw (excluding the screw threading).
- In hardwood, drill a small hole of the screw root diameter, called a pilot hole, about three quarters of the total thickness.
- In softwood, a bradawl can be used for small screws.
- A clearance hole will have to be drilled through the top member to accommodate traditional wood screws.

flared tip with hardened tip

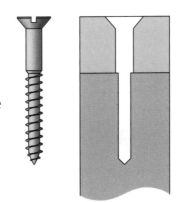

Clearance hole allows screw to pass through one of the pieces of wood.

Pilot hole allows screw to bite into wood without splitting it.

Top Tip
Always ensure that the screwdriver tip fits the screw head and that the tip is not worn or rounded before beginning.

Quick Test

1. What is the purpose of an oval brad?
2. Describe the use of a 'pilot hole' when fitting wood screws.

Flat-frame joints

Examples of Flat-frame joints

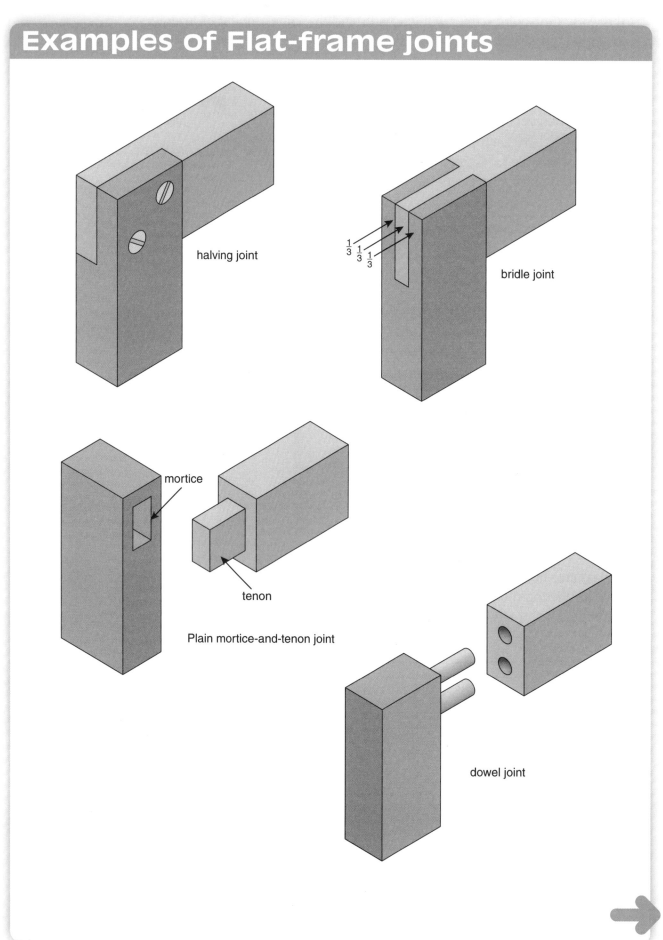

halving joint

bridle joint

$\frac{1}{3}$ $\frac{1}{3}$ $\frac{1}{3}$

mortice

tenon

Plain mortice-and-tenon joint

dowel joint

Dowelled joint

This is a very strong method of jointing, used mainly in factory-made furniture.

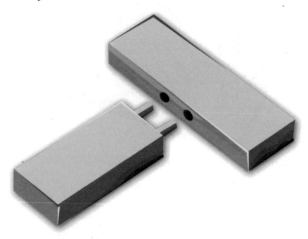

Mark each component to length, and sand the ends square on the belt/disc sander as for the **cross-halving** joint.

Marking the joint

The two halves of the joint are first clamped together vertically in the vice, with the two squared to be joined uppermost and flush with each other, as shown.

Mark and square the centre line of each dowel position across both parts.

Set the marking gauge to half the material thickness, and gauge on the centre line of each dowel from both sides.

Using a bradawl, make starting holes for the dowels where the gauge-lines cross.

Boring dowel holes

With a **dowel bit** inserted in the power drill, place the drill point on the marked position and, holding the drill absolutely vertically, drill the holes in turn to the required depth. (See p. 81, 'Dowel corner joint'.)

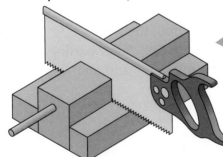

Top Tip
To make a jig for cutting dowels to length, drill a hole the size of the dowel in a piece of block and mark off the length to be cut. Then you can cut as many dowels as you need to an accurate length with square and even ends.

Quick Test

1. Give two reasons why the dowelled joint is used in factory-made furniture.

Answers 1 It is a very strong joint system. 2. It can be easily mass-produced.

Corner halving joint

This joint is one method of joining the corners of a flat frame (such as in the clock project on pp. 118–119).

Marking out the basic halving joint

A practice joint may be made from a single length. Mark out the position of the shoulder at each end, and make sure that the length of the lap matches the width of the material. Square the lines across the face side and down the edges.

Gauging the depth

Set the marking gauge to half the thickness of the wood and, working from the face side, gauge a line up both edges and across the end of both laps.

Cutting out the laps

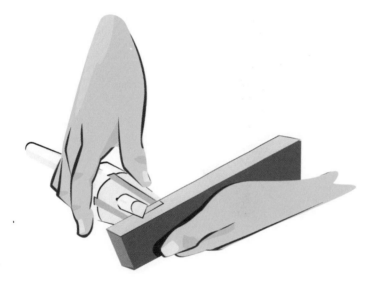

This is the same process as removing waste from the tee-halving joints and cutting a tenon (see pp. 36, 39). After parting off, the two halves of the joint should be fitted by hand and pressed together.

Top Tip

When sawing down to the waste side of a line, there should be no space between the saw-cut and the line. The teeth of the saw to one side should cut down the centre of the line, or just leave the line on.

Quick Test

1. What advantage would this joint have compared to a standard mitre joint?

Answers **1.** Because of the lap, it would have additional strength.

Mitred halving joint

A mitred halving joint is used in flat frames that are required to be more rigid. The corner mitre is also an attractive feature.

Marking a mitred corner

As before, a practice joint may be made from a single length. Setting a sliding bevel to the angle of 45 degrees or using a combination square, mark out the position of the angled shoulder at each end. Make sure the length of the lap matches the width of the material, and square the lines down the edges.

Gauging the depth

Setting the marking gauge to half the thickness, scribe a line from the face side on the inner edge of the joint and across the end grain.

Cutting the angled shoulder

Clamp the workpiece in the vice at an angle and saw down to the waste side of the gauge-line right to the shoulder line. With the work held firmly on the sawing board, saw down to the waste side of the angled shoulder to remove the waste. Clean out any roughness on the tenons, and fit the joint.

Top Tip
The angled shoulder can be cut using a mitre saw – after sawing down the tenon.

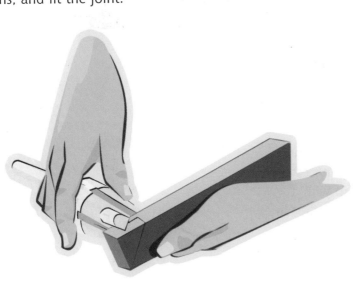

Quick Test

1. When sawing down to a gauge-line, why is it so important to stop exactly at that point?

Answer 1. If you saw down below the gauge-line, the joint will be weakened.

Tee-halving joint

Top Tip
Use a slicing action to smooth off the bottom of the notch, and check that it is level by using the long edge of the chisel.

Marking out the joint

Taking the sizes from the appropriate components (a practice joint may be made from a single length), square the shoulder-line and notch-lines all round. Set the marking gauge to half the material's thickness, and gauge all round the end as shown.

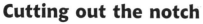

Cutting out the notch

Having sawn down carefully to the waste side of the gauge-line, remove the waste wood in stages, working from each side with the workpiece held firmly in the vice. Finish off the bottom of the notch carefully as shown.

Sawing the lap

With the work held firmly in the vice at an angle, saw down to the shoulder, keeping to the waste side of the gauge-line. Turn the work round and saw down the other edge, then finish off by sawing down squarely to the shoulder.

Removing the waste

With the workpiece resting in the sawing board, saw down the shoulder-line to remove the waste. If necessary, trim the shoulder square with the chisel or shoulder plane.

After parting off, the two halves of the joint should be fitted together by hand. If necessary, take a shaving off the side of the lap with a smoothing plane, and press gently together in the vice.

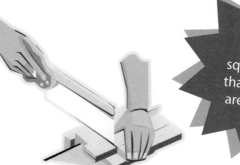

Top Tip
Use a try square to test that shoulders are square all round.

Quick Test

1. What is the main strength of this joint in a flat frame?

Answer 1. Used as a cross-member in a frame, it cannot be pulled out sideways.

Dovetail halving joint

Marking out the lap dovetail

As before, a practice joint may be made from a single piece of material. Having marked out and cut a lap at one end as described on page 34, use a **metal dovetail template** and a sharp pencil to mark the dovetail on the workpiece as shown.

Shaping the lap dovetail

Saw carefully down the short shoulders on both sides of the lap, then clamp the workpiece firmly in the vice and pare away the waste with a bevel-edged chisel to form the sloping sides of the dovetail.

Marking and cutting the shaped notch

Part off the length of material at its centre. Using the dovetail as a template, carefully mark the shoulders of the notch across the face side at the centre of the remaining half. Square the shoulder-lines down the sides, and, setting the marking gauge to half the thickness as before, gauge both edges from the face side between the lines and cut the notch as before.

The two halves of the joint should be fitted together by hand. If necessary, take a shaving off the side of the lap with a smoothing plane, and press gently together in the vice.

Top Tip
When paring down the sloping sides of the dovetail, rest an elbow on the bench for more support and control, and keep both hands behind the cutting edge.

Top Tip
Pay particular attention to the fitting of the stopped end.

Quick Test

1. Name the main advantage of using this joint.

Answer 1. The halving does not show on the end of the frame.

Stopped halving joint

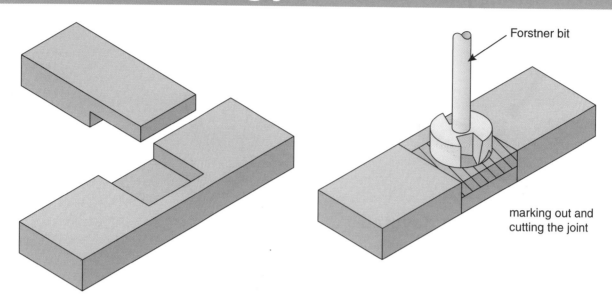

Forstner bit

marking out and
cutting the joint

Marking out the joint

A practice joint may be made from a single length. Mark out the position of the
parts in the same way as for the tee-halving joint, noting the shorter lap. Square
the shoulder-line and notch-lines all round. Set the marking gauge to half the
material's thickness, and gauge all round the end as shown and only one side
of the notch. Next, set the marking gauge to the size of the stopped part of the
notch, and gauge from the face edge.

Cutting out the notch

Having marked out the waste wood, mark the centre for drilling out the waste.
Fit a Forstner bit the size of the notch in the pedestal drilling machine set to
the notch depth. Drill out the notch carefully, and remove the remainder of the
waste by sawing down the notch-line to the waste side and gently paring with a
bevel-edged chisel.

Sawing the lap

With the work held firmly in the vice at an angle, saw down to the shoulder,
keeping to the waste side of the gauge-line. Turn the workpiece round and saw
down the other edge, then finish off by sawing down squarely to the shoulder
as before. (See p. 36, 'Tee-halving joint': 'Sawing the lap'.)

After parting off, the two halves of the joint should be fitted together by hand.
If necessary, take a shaving off the side of the lap with a smoothing plane, and
press gently together in the vice.

Stub-haunched mortice-and-tenon joint

Marking out the joint

A practice joint may be made from a single length of material. Mark out the shoulder of the stub tenon at one end to its length. Mark out the ends of the mortice, ensuring that the length of the mortice is the same as the material width, leaving approximately 25 mm for a horn at the end. Mark out the parting-off point in between. Mark and square across the haunch-line on the mortice. The haunch should be about one third of the mortice width. Square all four points carefully round the material.

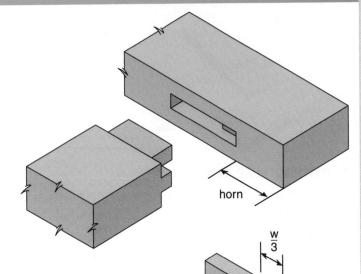

Marking on the mortice-and-tenon gauge-lines

Set the marking pins of the mortice gauge to the mortice chisel size, and follow the instructions for gauging the through mortice-and-tenon joint.

Cutting out the mortice

Follow the instructions for cutting out the through mortice on page 40, but this time only remove the waste of the stub mortice to the pre-determined depth, which is the length of the tenon. Next, remove the waste from the haunch to a depth of 7 mm. (You can go beyond the haunch-line into the horn.)

Sawing down the tenon

Follow the instructions for sawing down the through tenon on page 41. Place the joint firmly in a vertical position in the vice, and mark out the position of the haunch. Mark the 7 mm depth

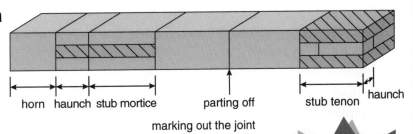

marking out the joint

up vertically from the shoulder, and square across. Measure the size of the haunch, and square or gauge down. Cut out the tenon haunch with the tenon saw.

After parting off, the two halves of the joint should be fitted together by hand. If necessary, trim off the tenon sides with the bevel-edged chisel, and press gently together in the vice.

Top Tip
To ensure tight fitting of the haunch, leave the haunch slightly long and pare down to fit.

Quick Test

1. What is the purpose of a haunch in this joint?

Answer 1 To prevent the frame from twisting.

Through mortice-and-tenon joint

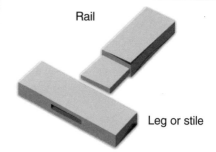

Rail

Leg or stile

Marking out the joint

A practice joint may be made from a single length of material. Mark the centre point of the material. Mark out the shoulder and ends of the mortice, ensuring that the length of the tenon is the same as the material's width. Square all three positions carefully round the material.

Marking on the mortice-and-tenon gauge-lines

Set the mortice-gauge marking pins to the size of the mortice chisel to be used by means of the end adjusting screw (see p. 13). Adjust the marking pins to the centre of the wood thickness by gauging dots from each side and adjusting. Gauging from the face side and, resting the end of the material on the bench, mark on each side of the joint, taking care not to slip beyond the shoulder and mortice lines.

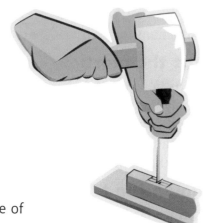

Cutting out the mortice

- Always secure the workpiece firmly, either in the vice or by clamping it to the bench on top of a piece of scrap wood, as shown.
- Hold the chisel vertically with your left hand as shown; or you can hold the blade for greater control.
- Carefully position the chisel between the mortice-gauge marks about 2 mm from the end of the mortice with the bevel away from you.
- Strike the handle of the chisel with a light tap from the side of the mallet. Move the chisel blade outwards and repeat, delivering only light taps to form a series of cuts along the length of the mortice.

Removing the waste

Stop about 2 mm from the other end (this is to protect against showing spaces outside the line), and, with the forefinger under the blade, carefully lever out the chippings from this first layer. Repeat this operation, keeping the chisel vertical at all times and only tapping lightly each time until you reach halfway down.

Note When forming a stub mortice and tenon, the depth can be measured with a rule and levelled off at this stage.

Through mortice and tenon

Pare the ends of the mortice square to the marked lines, then reverse the workpiece, knocking out the chippings. Repeat the process for a through mortice.

Sawing the tenon

With the work held firmly in the vice at an angle, so that the end-grain faces away from you, saw down to the shoulder, keeping to the waste side of each gauge-line. Turn the workpiece round, and saw down to the shoulder line on the other side of the tenon.

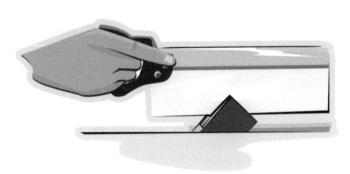

Cutting square

Clamp the workpiece upright and saw down, following the pre-sawn cuts to the shoulder-line.

Sawing the shoulders

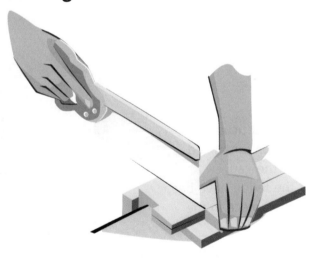

With the workpiece resting in the sawing board, saw down the shoulder-line to remove the waste. Make sure you keep the saw level and don't cut below the gauge-line. If necessary, trim the shoulder square with the chisel or shoulder plane, and fit the joint.

After parting off, the two halves of the joint should be fitted together by hand. If necessary, trim off the tenon sides with the bevel-edged chisel, and press gently together in the vice.

Top Tip
When cutting the tenon, always saw down the sides in the three stages first – then saw down the shoulders.

Quick Test

1. Why is it so important to hold the mortice chisel absolutely vertical when cutting a mortice?

Answer | 1 The mortice must be cut true so that the assembled frame will not be twisted.

Rebated mortice-and-tenon

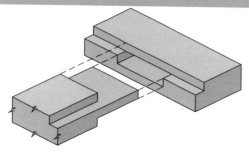

This is a joint system used in flat frames that are glazed or fitted with panels. This joint is sometimes called 'the advanced shoulder joint' but, apart from this alternative name, is really just a standard mortice and tenon.

Marking out the joint

A practice joint may be made from a single length of material already rebated. Mark out the twin shoulders of the tenon at one end, ensuring that the distance between them is the same as the depth of the rebate. Mark out the ends of the mortice, ensuring that the length of the mortice is the same as the material width. Mark out the parting-off point in between. Square all five points carefully round the material.

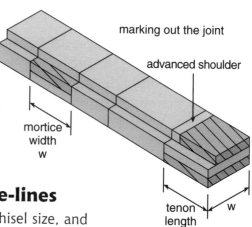

marking out the joint

advanced shoulder

mortice width w

tenon length w

Marking on the mortice-and-tenon gauge-lines

Set the marking pins of the mortice gauge to the mortice chisel size, and note that the mortice should be marked from the base of the rebate. Working from the face side, follow the instructions for gauging the through mortice-and-tenon joint.

Cutting out the mortice

Follow the instructions for cutting out the through mortice on p. 40, taking care when starting at the rebate.

Sawing down the tenon

Carefully mark out the waste wood on the tenon, paying particular attention to the advanced shoulder. Place the joint firmly in an angled position in the vice, and saw down to the waste side of the gauge-line. Repeat this process as before until both sides of the tenon have been sawn down to the different shoulder levels. Place the workpiece in the sawing board, and saw down the shoulders.

After parting off, the two halves of the joint should be fitted together by hand. If necessary, trim off the tenon sides with the smoothing plane, and press gently together in the vice.

Top Tip
If the advanced shoulder does not fit tightly into the rebate, gently run the tenon saw down the reverse shoulder.

Quick Test

1. Name a situation where this joint would be used.

Answer 1 For a frame where a glass or ply panel has to be fitted.

Bridle joint (or saddle-and-bridle) joint

Marking out the shoulders

A practice joint may be made from a single length. Mark the centre point of the material. Mark on the shoulder-line at the bridle end and the saddle notch-lines in the centre of the other part. Carefully square all the lines round the material.

Gauging the joint

Set the marking pins of the mortice gauge to the width of the mortice chisel, roughly one third of the thickness of the wood. Adjust the stock so that the pins make marks exactly in the centre. Working from the face side, gauge on lines round the end of the bridle part (at the end) and between the shoulder-lines on both sides of the saddle part. Mark out the waste wood.

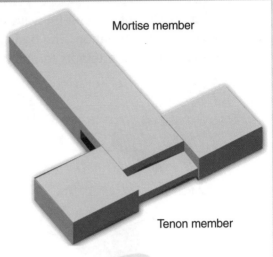

Mortise member

Tenon member

Cutting out the bridle

Cut the mortice part from both sides with the tenon saw as described for the tee-halving joint (see p. 36), but this time the waste wood is in the centre. Use a coping saw to remove the waste carefully. With a mortice chisel held vertically, trim down to the line on a chiselling board. (See p. 40, 'Cutting out the mortice'.)

Cutting the saddle part

On both sides of the saddle part, carefully saw the shoulders down to the waste side of the line to the gauge-lines, then make three or four similar cuts in between. With the work, held firmly in the vice, remove the waste wood in stages, working from each side. Finish off the bottom of the notch carefully as shown. (See p. 36, 'Tee-halving'.)

After parting off, the two halves of the joint should be fitted together by hand. If necessary, take a shaving off the side of the bridle part with a smoothing plane, and press together in the vice.

Top Tip
When chiselling out the waste, try using the heel of your hand to push the chisel, and rest the other elbow on the bench for greater control.

Top Tip
When cutting out the bridle (open mortice), ensure that the inside is completely free of rags to give a good fit.

Quick Test

1. Which part of this joint is called the saddle?   2. Which part of this joint is called the bridle?

Answers 1. The saddle is the part with the notch on either side. 2. The bridle is the open mortice part.

Single dovetail joint

There are a number of very useful ways to use the single dovetail joint, depending upon the situation. The basic principle is to form a joint of sufficient strength that will resist attempts to pull it apart.

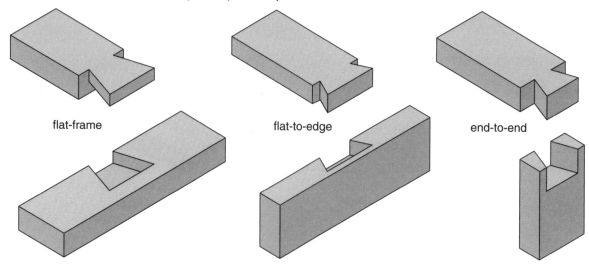

flat-frame   flat-to-edge   end-to-end

The quickest and easiest method of construction is the end-to-end dovetail. A practice joint may be made from a single length of material as before. Square both ends on the disc sanding machine. Set the marking gauge to the thickness of the material, and gauge all round from each end. Mark out the dovetail at one end using a **dovetail template**, measuring in about 5 mm from each side to start the line. Mark the waste wood.

Hold the material vertically in the vice and saw down the waste side of the dovetail lines to the shoulder-line. Hold the work in the sawing board, saw down the shoulders at each side and trim out any waste.

After parting off, and with the blank piece held vertically in the vice, place the dovetail on top at right angles and mark on the pins. After marking the waste wood, saw down the pins to the waste side of the line and remove the waste carefully with a coping saw. The bottom, between the pins, can be smoothed by vertical chiselling down to the gauge-line from both sides on a cutting board.

The two halves of the joint should be fitted together by hand. If necessary, place the pin end in the vice, and tap in the dovetail gently with a pin hammer, or press gently together in the vice.

Quick Test

1. Name two situations where this joint may be used.

Answers 1 In a mid-frame cross-member to stop the sides from pulling apart. **2.** To join the corners of a frame where the members are on edge.

Mitre tools

Mitre-saw jigs

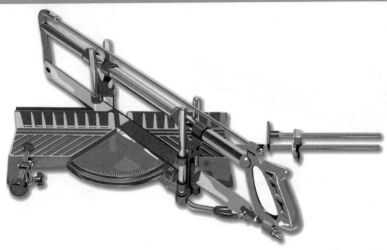

The mitre saw

The mitre-saw jig is used to cut small sections to a precise 45-degree mitre. The wide tensioned blade, with specially hardened teeth, slides within its own carriage and can be set to any angle between 45 degrees and 90 degrees. It can be moved by means of a **locking trigger** that locks the saw at any required angle. An adjustable stop end is also provided so that mitred lengths can be paired exactly.

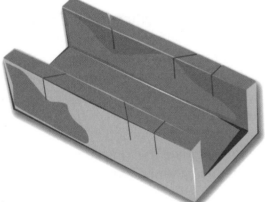

Top Tip
It is important to hold down, or clamp, both the mitre box and the mitre saw when in use. The mitre box is usually fitted with a strip underneath which can be clamped in the vice.

The mitre box

A traditional mitre box is usually constructed from beech with two raised edges (see illustration). The material to be mitred is held inside against the forward raised edge. After lining up to the measured mark, the tenon saw is inserted into one of the accurately formed slots, and the mitre is cut at exactly 45 degrees. After parting off, and with the blank piece held vertically in the vice, place the dovetail on top at right angles and mark on the pins. After marking the waste wood, saw down the pins to the waste side of the line and remove the waste carefully with a coping saw. The bottom, between the pins, can be smoothed by vertical chiselling down to the gauge-line from both sides on a cutting board.

Top Tip
To ensure accuracy when using either a mitre saw or block, lower the saw down carefully so that the nearest teeth are just on the line at the inside edge.

Quick Test

1. What is the main advantage of using a mitre-saw jig instead of a mitre block?

Answer 1 A mitre-saw jig can be quickly and accurately adjusted to different angles.

Mitred joint

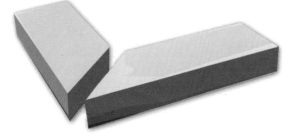

This is the classic joint for picture frames. The traditional method of cutting the mitre is the mitre box.

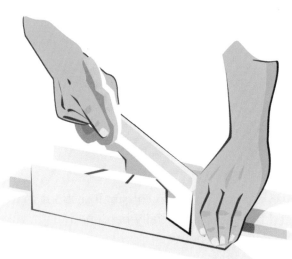

Cutting the joint using the mitre saw

On each piece of wood, mark out the total outside length of the frame. This is the distance between the long points of the mitre. Square these marks round the edge and insert the wood in the mitre box firmly against the back, gently moving the wood along until the long point is directly under the saw when lowered. Always saw to the waste side of the line so that you can just see the mark. Release the trigger and reverse the angle to 45 degrees on the other side of the scale, and repeat the process on the other end of the wood. You can now use this as a template for the opposite side, holding the long edges back to back, or set the stop end to the required length for cutting. (See p. 45, 'The mitre saw'.)

This process is repeated for the other two sides. Take care to match the pairs of sides exactly.

Top Tip
Cut the longest sides first, then if you make a mistake you can use these for the shorter ones.

Clamping the mitred frame using a cord mitre clamp

When gluing up, set the mitre-frame clamp to the required size on the bench on a board. Glue three sides of the frame and place them in the frame. Gluing and fitting in the fourth side should place some strain on the clamp. Ensuring that the corners are firmly located, tighten the clamp fully, taking care that no buckling takes place. Wipe off any surplus glue with a paper towel. When fixing a single mitre joint, a steel mitre clamp may be used.

Top Tip
To ensure the frame remains flat when clamped, place a small weight on each corner.

Quick Test

1. Where is this joint commonly used?   **2.** What is its main disadvantage?

Answers 1 It is used to make picture frames. 2. It needs to be fitted using a frame clamp.

Mitred bridle joint

Tenon member

Mortice member

Marking out the joint

The mitre joint is much stronger than the corner lap joint and has the added advantage of end-grain only showing on one side.

As before, a practice joint can be made from a single piece of material. After sanding each end on the belt sander, mark on the face side and face edge, and mark on the width of each part from each end and at the mid-point. Square these points all round the wood.

Mark on the 45-degree shoulder on both sides of each end with a **mitre square** or **combination square**.

Top Tip
Always gauge from the same face edge to ensure accurate joint fitting.

Gauging the tenon and open mortice

Set the distance between the pins of the mortice gauge to the size of the mortice chisel to be used, and adjust so that the pins are central. Gauge both ends and sides to the shoulder-lines, all from the face side. (See p. 40 for gauging a mortice-and-tenon joint.)

Cutting the open mortice

The open mortice is cut in the same way as the bridle joint (see p. 43). When the sides have been sawn down to the waste side of the line as shown, (remember the waste is in the centre) the waste is then removed with a coping saw and the bottom pared smooth from each side. The end is then sawn off to the marked angle.

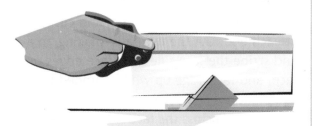

Saw down the shoulder-lines of the saddle part, and trim with a shoulder plane if necessary.

After parting off the two halves, the joint should be fitted by hand and trimmed off.

Quick Test

1. Where would this joint be used, and what is its main advantage?

Answer 1 It is used in larger flat frames of heavier sections to give extra strength at the corners.

Sequence of operations

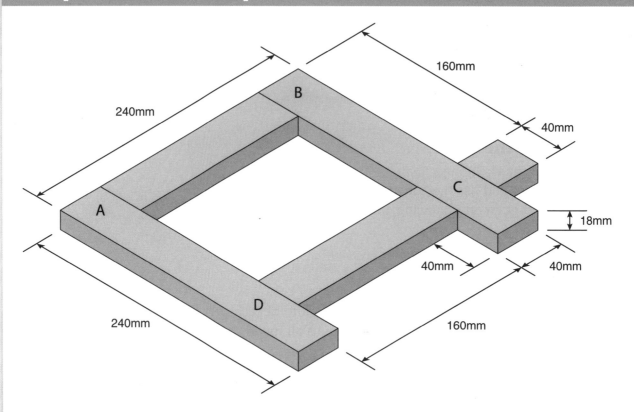

With reference to the illustration above, we will assume that the members AD and BC are the two vertical sides of a door frame, called **stiles**. The top and bottom rails would be AB and CD respectively. Because of the nature of the joints at A and B, we should leave the two stiles projecting around 40 mm at the top (not shown).

Marking out the stiles

Check the sizes of the material and cut two stiles, making an allowance for horns at each end. Cut the two rails, making an allowance for the horn at C. Select and scribe the face sides and face edges of each member. Pair the stiles face-to-face, and face edge up while clamped in the vice, and mark on the joint-lines, square across and square round for joints A, B and C, being careful to square the haunch-line across the face edge for joint B.

With reference to the through mortice-and-tenon joint at B (see p. 40) and the bridle joint at A (see p. 43), set the mortice gauge to the chisel size and, working from the face side, scribe along both edges between the joint-lines.

With the marking gauge set to half the thickness, again working from the face side, scribe between the joint-lines along both edges for joint C and the inside only for joint D (this will be the centre for the dowels).

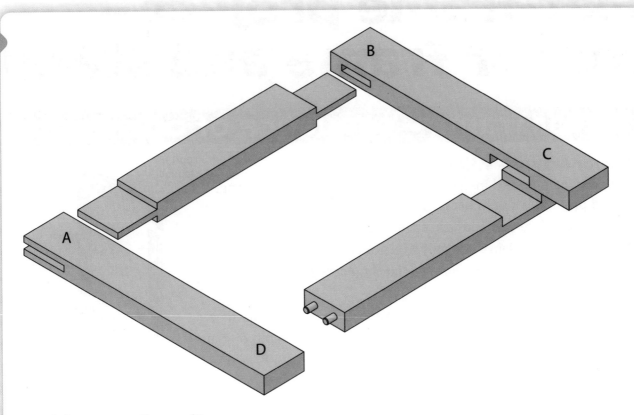

Marking out the rails

With the rails paired face-to-face and clamped in the vice flush at one end with the face edges up, mark on the shoulder-lines, remembering the two shoulder-lines for the cross-halving joint at C. After squaring the shoulder-lines all round, again working from the face side, scribe on the tenons all round at either end of the top rail AB with the mortice gauge. With the marking gauge still set, scribe on the depth of the halving joint and the centre-line for the dowels at D.

Cutting the mortices

The mortices and haunch can be cut either by hand or using the mortice machine. With either process, care must be taken to keep the mortices vertical and not to cut beyond the ends of the mortices, where the cut will show.

Cutting the tenons

Saw down to the waste side of the tenons and then saw across the shoulder, as described on page 41.

Framing and fitting

In the case of a practice frame, it is not necessary to glue and clamp. The joints should be fitted individually, taking care to square the frame as described on p. 26.

Top Tip
If a tenon shoulder is not squeezing up tight, and there is a gap on one side, run the tenon saw carefully down the shoulder on the opposite side, making sure not to cut the tenon.

Quick Test

1. Why is it important to mark on the face side and the face edge on all frame members?

Answer 1 These are reference surfaces, e.g. always gauge from the face side so that the resulting frame is not twisted. The face edge should always be to the inside of the frame.

Flat-frame project – mirror frame and stand

Mirror frame – sequence of operations

Mirror frame – stiles

- Check the prepared material sizes against the working drawing, and plane to width as necessary.
- Mark on a face side and face edge on all components.
- Cut the stiles to length, slightly oversize part A.
- Pair the stiles and mark out the joint shoulders and the exact lengths.
- Square the shoulders all round.
- Cut and square the ends to length on a belt-disc sanding machine.
- Set the marking gauge to half-thickness, and gauge depth of joints from the faceside.
- Saw down the shoulders of the lap notches.
- Cut out the notches (see p. 38, 'Stopped halving joint').
- Saw down the half-tenons of the stopped lap housing (see p. 38).
- Saw down the shoulders of the stopped lap housing.
- Clean out and smooth the joints.

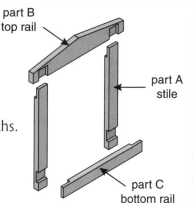

part B
top rail

part A
stile

part C
bottom rail

Mirror frame – rails

- Cut the rails to length, slightly oversize parts B and C.
- Pair the top and bottom rails, parts B and C, and mark on their lengths and joint shoulder-lines.
- Square all round.
- Mark out the top shaping on part B.
- Set the marking gauge to half the thickness, and gauge the lap-joint depths from the face side – part A.
- Set the marking gauge to stopped lap-joint length, and gauge on the top rail from the face edge – part B.
- Saw down the half-tenons of part C (see p. 38).
- Saw down the shoulders of part C and clean out the joint.
- Using an appropriately-sized Forstner bit in a pedestal drilling machine, drill out the stopped lap housing to depth on part B.
- Carefully saw down the sides of the stopped lap housing and cut the joint (see p. 38).
- Saw to the waste side of the sloping lines using a portable jig-saw on part B.
- Holding part B in the vice so that the sloping line is level, plane carefully down to the line, planing from the apex.
- Check the alignment of all shoulders by pairing stiles A and rails B and C.
- Carefully number both corresponding parts of each joint in places where the numbers will not be planed off.
- Clean off the inside edges of all frame components with a smoothing plane.

Top Tip
When cutting menkers to length, make them slightly oversize to allow for sanding ends square.

Forming an edge rebate

With narrow strip material, such as a mirror frame, it is better to run the rebate with the wood clamped in the vice with the face edge up and face side away from you. The rebate plane can be set to the rebate width, usually the thickness of the mirror plate. The depth stop can be set to around 8 mm. The width and depth of the rebate can be lightly scribed with a marking gauge to form a guide. Holding the fence of the rebate plane against the back side, start from the end furthest from you and work backwards taking smooth strokes, finishing off with a final smooth stroke from end to end.

Forming a stopped-edge rebate

The process is the same as with an edge rebate, only the stopped end of the rebate must be made first, either by hand or with the mortice machine. The stopped ends of the rebate should be long enough to allow the rebate plane to finish the job.

Frame assembly

The flat frame can now be assembled, glued and clamped as described on pages 26 and 27.

Flushing off the frame

With the frame clamped flat on the bench, the work can be planed lightly to remove any pencil marks and any members that are projecting slightly. During this operation, it is important to hold the frame firmly – a piece of scrap wood held vertically in the vice below the frame level helps. Using a finely set smoothing plane, take even shavings off, starting in places where a member is projecting. It is important not to plane across the grain of any part, so great care should be taken not to leave plane marks.

This process should be repeated on the reverse side.

Top Tip
If the first shaving is rough, try adjusting the cutting iron back slightly, or re-set the width fence and plane from the other face.

Quick Test

1. Why is it important to check the material sizes against the working drawing?

Answer 1 So that you start with the right quantity and correct size of material.

Mirror frame – sequence of operations

Forming a chamfer

Set the marking gauge to the size of the chamfer, and gauge very lightly along the face and edge to be chamfered, so that you have a guide-line on both edges. To form a chamfer, place the workpiece firmly in the vice, with the edge to be worked projecting level about 50 mm above the bench surface. Holding the jack plane at an angle of 45 degrees, plane evenly along the entire length of the material until the guide marks have been reached. If the forming chamfer appears rough, try planing from the other end. (See p. 51, 'Forming an edge rebate'.)

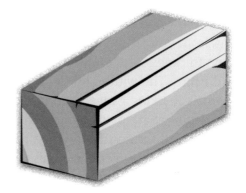

To form a chamfer to the angled top of the flat frame, hold the frame in the vice with the edge level and proceed as described above. Repeat the process for the other side.

Sanding the frame

The frame-sanding operation should be performed while the frame is lying flat, and immediately after flushing off both sides.

If sanding by hand, a sanding cork should be used and a circular motion used at all corner joint-lines, taking care not to scratch the surface by drawing the sandpaper across the grain.

Alternatively, a portable orbital sanding machine could be used with appropriate dust extraction.

Top Tip
When holding the plane at the desired angle, lock the wrist and hold the toe of the plane underneath, well clear of the blade, with a finger acting as a steady guide.

Fitting the mirror

The mirror can be fitted into the rebate by two methods:

1. If the depth of the rebate is the same as the thickness of the mirror, a face-fitted ply or MDF back can be used.

2. If the rebate is to the front face, allowance should be made for fitting **glazing beads**.

Top Tip
When sanding the face of the frame, care should be taken not to overlap the sandpaper on to the chamfer. This feature should be left sharp and not rounded.

Mirror stand – sequence of operations

Stand feet
- Check the prepared material sizes against the working drawing, and plane to width as necessary.
- Mark on the face side and face edge on all components.
- Cut the feet to length, slightly oversize part B.
- Pair the feet and mark out the joint shoulders, the taper and the exact lengths.
- Square the joint lines all round.

Stand uprights
- Check the prepared material sizes against the working drawing, and plane to width as necessary.
- Mark on the face side and face edge on all components.
- Pair the uprights and mark out the joint shoulders, the taper and the exact lengths.
- Square the joint lines all round.
- Set the marking pins of the mortice gauge to the size of the mortice chisel to be used, and gauge on the tenon, round the end from the face side (see page 39, Forming a mortice and tenon).
- With the same setting, gauge on the mortice top and bottom, between the lines from the face side.
- Cut the taper to the waste side of the line on all four parts A and B, using a portable jig-saw.
- Positioning each of the tapered parts in the vice so that the cut-line is level, plane down to the pencil line with the jack plane.

Cutting the mortice-and-tenon joints
- With the foot part held firmly in the vice, cut out the mortice on both feet from both sides with the appropriate mortice chisel and mallet.
- With part A held at an angle in the vice, cut down to the waste side of the gauge-line.
- Reverse the position and cut down the other side, and saw down level to the shoulder-line with the joint held vertically in the vice. Repeat the process for the other foot.
- Both joints can be fitted initially by hand and any adjustments made at this stage.
- Applying glue sparingly to both tenons, press home the joints. Checking for a square fit, clamp each complete end in a sash clamp. Wipe off any surplus glue with a paper towel.

The frames can be flushed off with a smoothing plane when the glue is set.

Mark the position of the swivel holes at the top of the upright, and drill through the holes with both ends clamped together.

Top Tip
It is good practice to match the ends together for an alignment check; and they may even be clamped in the same sash clamp with a sheet of polythene between them.

Diagram labels: part A upright, part B foot, part C rail, part D dowels

Quick Test
1. What tool would be used to form a chamfer?

Answer | 1 | A bench or hand plane.

Mirror stand – sequence of operations

Connecting rail

- Check the prepared material sizes against the working drawing, and plane to width as necessary.
- Mark on the face side and face edge.
- Cut the rail to length, slightly oversize part C.
- Square one end on the disc sanding machine, mark and square across the exact length, and sand to size on the machine.

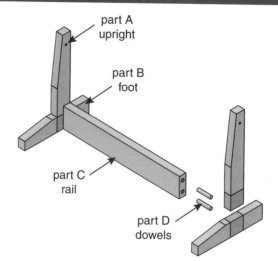

part A
upright

part B
foot

part C
rail

part D
dowels

Forming the dowel joints

- Carefully mark the position of the dowels on each end of the rail, gauging a line down the centre to give an accurate position (see p. 33, 'Dowelled joint').
- With the rail held vertically down in the vice, drive in a panel pin on both dowel positions.
- Using pliers or end-cutters, snip off the point of each pin. Repeat at the other end.
- Carefully place the end of each rail on the exact location, and press the pins into the ends. (See p. 33 on forming a dowel joint.)
- Carefully extract the locating panel pins.
- Set up the pedestal drilling machine for the next operation and perform safety checks under supervision.
- Using a dowel drill in the chuck, with the rail held perfectly vertical in a machine vice on the table of the drilling machine, drill down each end to a pre-determined depth on each dowel position. Repeat the process on the other end.
- Set up the pedestal drilling machine for the next operation (below) and perform safety checks under supervision.
- Using the same dowel drill in the chuck, with the end frame held on the table of the drilling machine, drill down each dowel position to a pre-determined depth. Repeat the process on the other end frame.
- After applying glue sparingly and inserting prepared dowels into each hole, the complete assembly can be placed in a prepared sash clamp with blocks and tested for square. Wipe off any surplus glue with a paper towel.

Top Tip
It is better to perform this operation with the rail and end assembly held flat on the bench while bringing the parts together.

Assembly of frame and stand

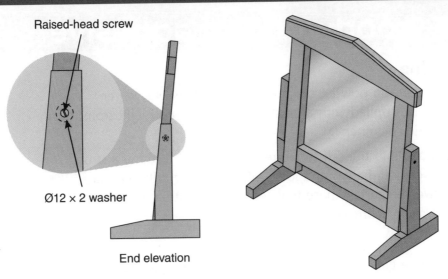

Raised-head screw

Ø12 × 2 washer

End elevation

Levelling the stand

If the stand appears to rock slightly when placed firmly on a flat board, this is a sign that there is a twist in the frame. To rectify this, place a pencil flat on the board and, holding the stand steady, scribe a pencil line along the length of the foot that is out of line. The underside of the foot member can then be planed down to the line to make the stand stable.

Assembly of frame and stand

- Ensure that the frame fits between the stand uprights with sufficient clearance to allow free movement.
- Mark the position of swivel fixings on the sides of the frame, allowing for clearance when the frame is vertical.
- Form a small hole with a bradawl for fixing screws at each marked position.
- Drive in a dome-head screw and washer through the prepared holes in the uprights into the screw holes, with an appropriate thickness of washer fitted between the frame and the upright. Tighten the screw sufficiently to allow the frame to be held in a tilted position.

Quick Test

1. Why is it important to lightly dress off and finish the face edges of a frame before final assembly?

Answer   1 The face edges will be the inside edges and are difficult to finish when assembled.

Glues and gluing

Types of woodworking adhesive

Woodworking glue

Supplied in liquid form, or as a powder or granules for mixing with water, woodworking glues can be applied with a brush or spreader, or straight from the nozzle of a tube or plastic container.

All adhesives are absorbed into the cell structure of the wood, forming a strong link between the fibres of both halves of a joint. Woodworking adhesives are divided roughly into two categories; those that set by evaporation, and those that set by means of a chemical reaction.

PVA glue

Commonly known as white glue, **polyvinyl-acetate** (PVA) glue is a popular and convenient adhesive for joint-making. It is supplied ready mixed in plastic bottles that are commonly fitted with a long nozzle for reaching into joint corners. PVA sets by evaporation, is non-toxic so it is safe to work with in a school workshop, and is almost clear when dry. Final adjustments can be made in joint-fitting thanks to the relatively slow setting time of PVA.

General-purpose PVA glue is only suitable for interior work. Although PVA forms a strong bond, the glue-line remains relatively flexible and may move slightly under conditions of stress. PVA does not sand well, as the friction causes the glue to soften and clog the sandpaper. **Chemical-bonding**, 'cross-linking' PVA glue is the most water-resistant of the PVA glues and forms an exceptionally strong bond.

Top Tip
When joining two pieces together using PVA glue, gently rub both together after application.

Urea and resin adhesives

Urea-formaldehyde-resin glue is a two-part adhesive that sets by chemical reaction. It is an excellent water-resistant adhesive that dries with a hard glue-line. The resin and hardener are usually supplied pre-mixed as dry powders that are activated when mixed with water. The mixture remains workable for about twenty minutes.

With some urea glues, the resin is supplied with a separate liquid hardener. The resin can be applied to one half of the joint, and the hardener to the other, and the glue only begins to set when the joint is assembled.

Hide glue

This is a traditional wood glue, made from animal skins and bones. Hide glue is non-toxic and sets by evaporation. Its main disadvantage is its strong smell and the fact that it has to be heated in a special glue pot placed over a burner. Synthetic resin adhesives have superseded hide glue.

Applying woodworking glue

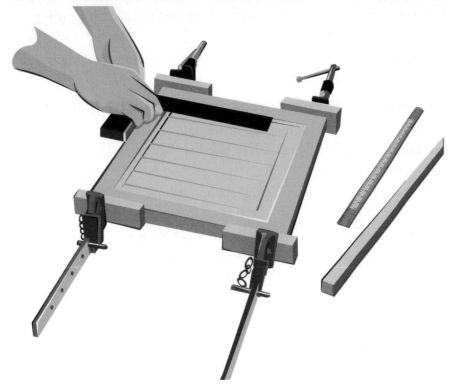

Preparation of the joints

Joints should be made to fit well, rather than relying on the glue to fill any gaps between the parts of the joint.

It is important that joints are cleaned out thoroughly and are free from chippings or dust. It is also important to work in a warm atmosphere, as cool conditions can cause the glue to 'chill' and set too quickly.

Apply the glue in a thin layer. If a nozzle is used, a thin piece of scrap wood can be used to spread the glue evenly over each part of the joint.

Take care to pay particular attention to coating the surface of the tenon, right into the shoulders, as most of the glue applied to the tenon is wiped off as the joint is assembled.

Don't rush when gluing up, but work as quickly as practicable in order to assemble joints before the wood begins to swell and the glue begins to gel.

Top Tip

Remember: every spillage of glue on the wood may leave a mark on the finished surface – so clean off all surplus glue immediately.

Quick Test

1. Name three advantages of using PVA glue in a school workshop.
2. Why is general-purpose PVA glue unsuitable for outdoor work?
3. Why is urea-formaldehyde glue suitable for outdoor work?
4. What are the main disadvantages of hide glue?

Answers 1 It is easy to apply from a bottle or tube. It does not set quickly, giving time to assemble parts. It does not stain clothes and so can be removed easily. 2. Because it is not usually waterproof. 3. Because it is waterproof and weatherproof. 4. It smells and needs to be heated in a special gluepot. It is not waterproof.

Assembling and gluing a simple flat-frame

Assembling and gluing a flat-frame structure successfully depends upon learning and using the processes outlined here.

Before assembling the members of a frame, lightly clean off all internal edges with the smoothing plane, and sand smooth.

Checking and matching the corresponding joint halves

After making sure that each joint fits square and true, lay out the stiles and rails end-to-end on the bench with the mating halves together. Number all mating joints, and check that they run in sequence.

Clear the bench of all tools not required for the clamping operation, and set out a board across the bench to carry the frame and keep it straight.

Set out two sash clamps with protective blocks across the bench on a board, as shown. Fully unwind the screw thread on the clamp and set the retaining steel pins (or bolts) so that they will accommodate the frame and blocks with some clearance to spare.

It is important that the frame is assembled initially without glue. This is called 'dry framing'. It will allow you to ensure that the joints are all within tolerance and flush with the face, and that the frame is square to the eye. It will also allow you to set the clamps and blocks to the required setting so that they can be adjusted quickly to the frame. Glue and wet paper towels should also be to hand so that you can concentrate on working without rushing around to find things.

Top Tip
If a joint shows a gap on one side when dry clamped, run the tenon saw carefully down the tight joint-line on the reverse side.

Holding the stile firmly in the vice with the inside edge facing up, apply glue sparingly to the tenons at the shoulders and into their mating mortices. Press each rail home by hand. Place the other stile over the mating tenons and gently tap the frame together with a mallet and protective scrap of wood.

Aligning the clamps

Place the frame on the bars and apply the clamps with protection blocks at each joint.

Ensure that the frame is square by testing each corner with the try square on the inside.

Set the frame in the sash clamps with the protective glue-blocks in place. This process is best carried out with two people, one at each side of the bench. Ensuring that the sash clamps run along the centre of the frame rails, gently tighten up the clamps until the joint shoulders close tight. As the glue seeps out, wipe the surplus off with a paper towel and don't forget to do the same on the reverse side.

Making pinch rods

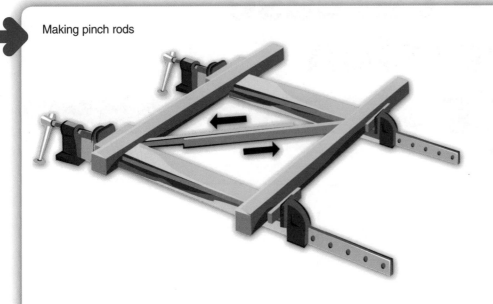

Checking for square

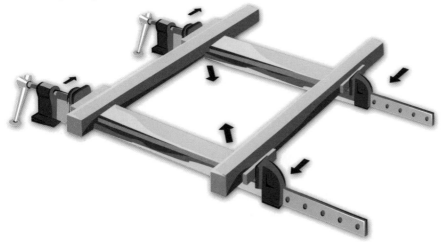

Checking for square

Before the glue has dried, you must check to see if the frame is square and flat. To check this, you can use some of the simple techniques already discussed.

If the frame is found to be off-square, slacken off the clamps a little and move them slightly to pull the frame square.

When checking the diagonals with a pointed rod, make a mark on the rod at the inside corner of each diagonal. Then make a mark midway between these two marks. Now adjust the clamps so that each diagonal comes to this centre mark.

Quick Test

1. Why is it necessary to have one person either side of the bench when clamping a flat frame?

Answer 1 To handle and fit the sash clamps and to move them when squaring.

Unit 2 – Carcase Construction

The carcase

What is a carcase?

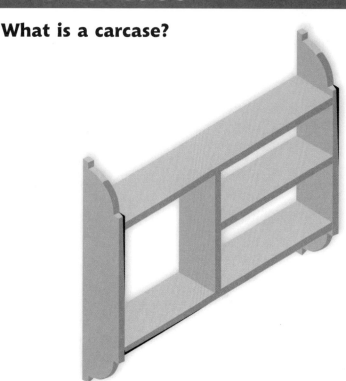

For the purposes of this course, a carcase is defined as a timber box whose four sides consist of material which is on edge and no less than around 100 mm wide, such as a wooden chest, drawer housing or cabinet structure.

This unit of the course has been designed to incorporate a wide range of woodworking processes appropriate to carcase construction.

Carcase construction also provides you with the opportunity to accumulate knowledge, understanding and skills fundamental to practical woodworking. You will be encouraged to be independent and to make your own choices in the use of both man-made and natural construction materials, giving full consideration to their properties and appropriate use.

You will produce a range of finished carcase joints which should be retained for assessment. The culmination of this unit is the manufacture of a carcase project, and generally the best joint will be considered for assessment.

While this unit may be taught sequentially, the final project should be considered at an early stage. You will be encouraged to practise the relevant joints and the use of materials and processes that will be appropriate to the manufacture of the final project.

What you will learn

Selecting woodworking materials for a specific purpose

You will learn to identify, and will be tested on, a range of woodworking materials and their properties. You will select construction materials that are appropriate for a given purpose. This will include a limited range of hard and soft woods, hardboard, MDF, interior and exterior ply, chipboard and blockboard. You will become familiar with their properties and working qualities.

Making a range of woodworking joints

You will learn, and be tested on, the marking-out and manufacture within tolerance of a range of woodworking joints relating to carcase construction. This will include butt joints, corner rebates, and through and stopped housings. You will also learn the correct terminology used when referring to tools and processes. The range of woodworking joints contained in this guide is appropriate for Intermediate 2 level.

Manufacturing a product from a working drawing

You will manufacture a carcase product from a working drawing. You will learn the practical use of creating a cutting list from the working drawing provided and of checking materials against it. You will learn to set out components, using rods and templates to within specified tolerance. You will learn to manufacture a product within tolerance. This will include the selection and use of appropriate joints and carcase assembly, including squaring and cramping.

You will also learn, and be tested on, all current health and safety regulations with regard to school workshop practice and safety legislation.

Top Tip
This is the time to bring your log book up to date, entering the tools, joint systems and materials you have used so far.

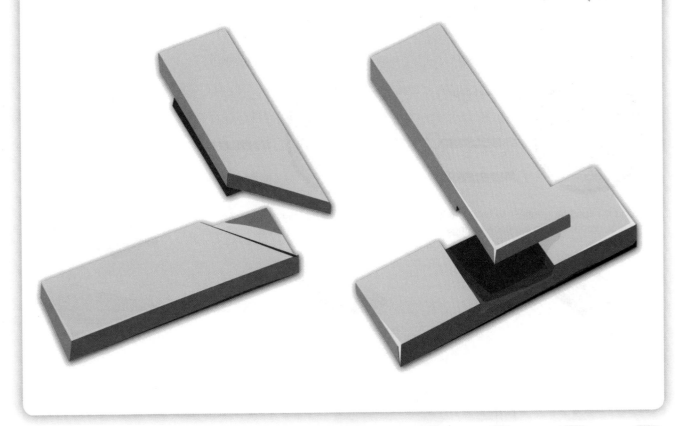

Natural materials (wood)

Man-made and natural materials

Hardwoods and softwoods: the main difference

In general, for commercial purposes, softwoods come from cone-bearing or evergreen trees, pine being an example. Hardwoods generally come from deciduous or broad-leafed trees – they shed their leaves in winter – an example being European oak. These are a useful convention but cannot be taken literally in all cases.

Preparation of material

All natural timber you will use in joints and project work will be machined on all surfaces and should be left slightly bigger to allow you to plane the finished product to the specified size.

Defects in wood

The main defects in wood are knots, which are merely the remains of a branch where it grew from the trunk. Knots, however, can be attractive in some woods if they can be planed easily and do not cause a weakness. Rough-cut timber must have the moisture removed from its cell structure before it is useful, by a process called seasoning. All timber for internal use has to have its moisture content reduced to approximately that of the interior where it is to be used, otherwise it would shrink and warp (twist). On the other hand, if wood is too dry, it will swell if used in a damp situation. An external door may jam in wet weather if it is not protected.

How wood can move when cut

How wood warps

plain sawn (also known as flat sawn)

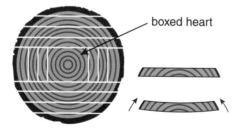

boxed heart

Wood is sliced tangentially to rings. As it shrinks, wood cups in direction of rings.

appearance of board

quarter cut (also known as rift sawn)

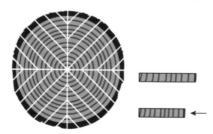

Wood is sliced radially to rings. As it shrinks, wood stays relatively flat.

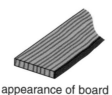

appearance of board

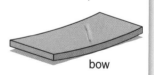

bow

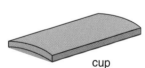

cup

spring

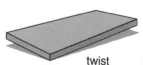

twist

Common softwoods

Redwood or European red pine

Mainly from Scandinavia or Russia, red pine can be anything from pale yellow to orange or light brown in colour, with distinctive growth rings. This wood can be resinous but is generally easy to plane and work.

Common uses

Depending on the grade and quality, red pine can be used for a wide range of projects from high-class joinery to construction work. Red pine is commonly used in school workshops.

Main advantages

Knots can be decorative, rarely fall out, and can be planed easily. It generally has straight grain, and the best grade does not twist easily.

Scots Fir or white pine

Produced in Scotland and other European countries, white pine can be very resinous and will warp and twist readily. The grain can be very stringy and wavy with hard knots, and it can be difficult to plane and work. It tends to be less expensive than red pine.

Top Tip

When selecting strip boards, look for lengths with straight parallel grain.

Common uses

White pine is used mainly for rough exterior construction work including telegraph poles, fences, gates, moulds or formwork for concrete work and general exterior carpentry, but it is also used for strip flooring and internal partitions.

Quick Test

1. Describe the main differences between softwoods and hardwoods.

2. Why is it better to have your strip material supplied with the breadth and thickness slightly bigger?

3. What is the purpose of seasoning?

4. What are the main advantages that red pine has over white pine in furniture construction?

Answers 1 Softwoods generally come from coniferous trees, and hardwoods generally come from deciduous trees. 2. So that the finished work can be dressed off and still be within tolerance. 3. To adjust the moisture content in wood to that of the situation where it will be used so that it does not shrink or swell. 4. The knots can be planed easily because they are softer than white pine knots.

Common hardwoods

Hardwoods can be very hard (greenheart, for example, was used to make fishing rods and is a particularly hard and tough wood) or extremely soft (obeche and balsa wood are both hardwoods). Some hardwoods are so heavy that they are unable to float in water – *Lignum vitae*, for example, was used for bearings in ships' propeller shafts.

Mahogany

The most common hardwood used in schools today is mahogany, which comes from Central and South America. It is a pale red or brown wood, often with no obvious or marked grain structure, but tends to be quite strong and stable. Mahogany is generally easy to plane and work in strip form. This wood stains and polishes well, but good quality is becoming rare and therefore expensive. Although the cost of mahogany is rising, substitutes with a similar colour and grain structure are available.

Mahogany

The main advantages of mahogany are that it has an attractive grain structure, with very few knots. It tends to have a mild even grain in the best grades and is relatively free from warping and twisting if well seasoned. Its main disadvantage, apart from the high cost, is that some boards can be very difficult to plane due to rotary grain structure.

Common uses

Mostly used for internal joinery, furniture, doors and windows.

Beech

West African beech is a fairly hard and even, close-grained wood which is supplied either steamed (sterilised to stop it discolouring) or unsteamed (white beech). Because of its hardness, it requires a well-sharpened plane to work well.

Beech

Common uses

Beech is used extensively for bench stops, mallets, sawing and chiselling boards, some tool handles, protective inserts in woodworking vices, and many other items. It is fairly easy to work, but a well-sharpened cutting edge is required.

Oak

North American oak is pale to mid-brown in colour and quite different from European oak, which is easier to plane and work and a little browner in tone. Oak stains and polishes well, but iron will react to the acid in the timber and cause staining, so brass or stainless steel screws and fittings must be used.

Oak

Common uses

Oak was traditionally used for making barrels. It is now used for making top-quality furniture.

Walnut

American walnut is dark brown, almost purple in colour whereas European walnut is a mid- to dark brown in colour with thin black streaks. Both varieties are becoming rare and therefore very expensive. This wood generally works well, but care should be taken when planing it, as some grains run in a wavy or rotary direction.

Walnut

Common uses

Used extensively for quality furniture and cabinet making.

Top Tip
Most common European hardwoods come from deciduous trees i.e. trees that decide to shed their leaves in winter.

Quick Test

1. Why is hardwood preferred when making quality furniture?
2. Why is pine being used more and more in schools and colleges?
3. What wood is used for making mallets and tool handles? Give reasons why.
4. What are the main things you would look for in top-quality furniture?

Answers 1 Because it is hard-wearing and strong and has a pleasing colour and grain. 2. Because hardwood is becoming very scarce and therefore expensive. 3. Usually beech because it is hard-wearing and relatively free from knots. 4. Good appearance, functional, strong and stable in use.

Man-made boards

Manufactured boards are commonly used in most internal joinery and cabinet-making situations. Their main advantage is that they can cover wide areas and are not subject to warping to the same extent as natural timber. Manufactured boards are generally used for interior work, but **resin** and **phenol-bonded** boards are manufactured for exterior and marine use.

Plywood

Plywood consists of several thin layers of wood, usually with the grain at right angles in alternate layers. This is sometimes called crossply. It is not usually subject to shrinkage, is very strong in panel form and costs less than natural wood. It is supplied in useful thicknesses ranging from 3 mm to 25 mm. Decorative ply has a veneer of decorative hardwood bonded to one or both sides and is perfect for enclosed panels and carcase construction.

Blockboard

The inside core of blockboard is made from solid strips of softwood glued along their edges. It is faced with a layer of veneer on each side. Blockboard is comparably lighter than plywood, resistant to bending, and is used for large structures and shelving. It is normally available in 19 mm and 25 mm thicknesses.

Laminboard

Similar to blockboard, laminboard has an internal core made of much smaller strips of softwood. As a result, the board is more stable in larger areas.

Particle boards

In particle boards, no thin layers of wood are used at all. Instead, the board is made up of small particles of processed timber bonded together with resin. Chipboard is the most common type, and is used as a base for laminated work such as Formica or wood veneer, or for low-cost shelving or carcase work. It has a smooth, hard surface and a softer core, and is prone to splitting when screws are driven into the edge.

Pineboard

Pineboard is like the core of blockboard but without the outer layers. Small strips of pine are glued together on edge and sanded smooth, making it ideal for instant shelving, carcase construction and the manufacture of low-cost furniture.

Fibreboards

Wood is shredded into a fibrous form and bonded with resin under high pressure to manufacture various forms of fibreboard. Softboard, or insulating board, is extremely light and soft and can be used as insulating material or as a pinboard. Hardboard has one hard surface only, but is very stable and bends easily. The main disadvantage of hardboard is that it will buckle if exposed to damp conditions. It is useful in the workshop for making templates. Tempered hardboard is impregnated with resins to make it more water-resistant.

Plastic laminate board

Increasingly, boards are being manufactured with a hard plastic laminate coating. This is very useful for kitchen work surfaces, shelving, certain types of wall panelling and laminate flooring. The main advantage of these boards is that they provide a hard, durable surface that is easy to clean.

MDF

MDF (Medium Density Fibreboard) is by far the most commonly used fibreboard product. It is dense, flat, stiff, has no knots and is easy to cut. It is prone to warping. The fibres are compressed so finely that it can be cut and shaped without crumbling. MDF is available in decorative form with real hardwood veneers already bonded to both faces.

HDF

HDF (High Density Fibreboard) is manufactured using very high pressure and is impregnated with resins to make it moisture-resistant. A good example is waterproof laminate flooring for kitchens and bathrooms.

Top Tip
Always wear a mask when sanding the edges of MDF, as it creates fine dust particles that can be dangerous if inhaled for any length of time.

Quick Test

1. Describe the structure of plywood.
2. What is the difference between blockboard and laminboard?
3. Name a popular use for chipboard. What is the main disadvantage of chipboard?
4. What is the main disadvantage of working with MDF?

Answers 1 Plywood is constructed using thin layers of wood with the grain laid in alternating directions. This creates a stiff board that will not twist and warp. **2.** Blockboard consists of a core of solid softwood strips faced with a veneer on both faces. Laminboard is similar to blockboard, but the strips in the core are narrower and usually of harder wood, so laminboard is a much stronger board. **3.** Used for general rough carcase construction, such as shelves etc. Can be finished with a plastic coating. Main disadvantage – cannot drive nails or screws into the board ends because of splitting of the particles. **4.** When machined, the dust caused is very fine and can be a health hazard if protection or dust-extraction is not used.

Projects using carcase construction

Examples

Wall cabinet

A wall-mounted cabinet with an open front and decorative shaping to the ends at top and bottom.

Kitchen wall unit

Open-fronted, wall-mounted shelf unit.

CD cabinet

A tall cabinet with flutes inserted internally to accommodate a number of compact discs. Can be constructed with a single column or multiple columns with grooves for CDs.

Bathroom cabinet

A wall-mounted cabinet with grooved mirror doors constructed in either hardwood or softwood.

Top Tip
Make some freehand sketches of carcase structures to familiarise yourself with their construction.

Storage chest

A box construction with a hollow lid incorporating plank construction.

Hobbies box

A box construction in hardwood or softwood with rebated top and bottom, incorporating one, or two, lift-out work trays.

Handy jewellery case

A box construction in hardwood or softwood with rebated bottom, incorporating housed-in partitions as required.

Quick Test

1. Describe the difference between a carcase and a flat frame.

Carcase joints

Examples of carcase joints

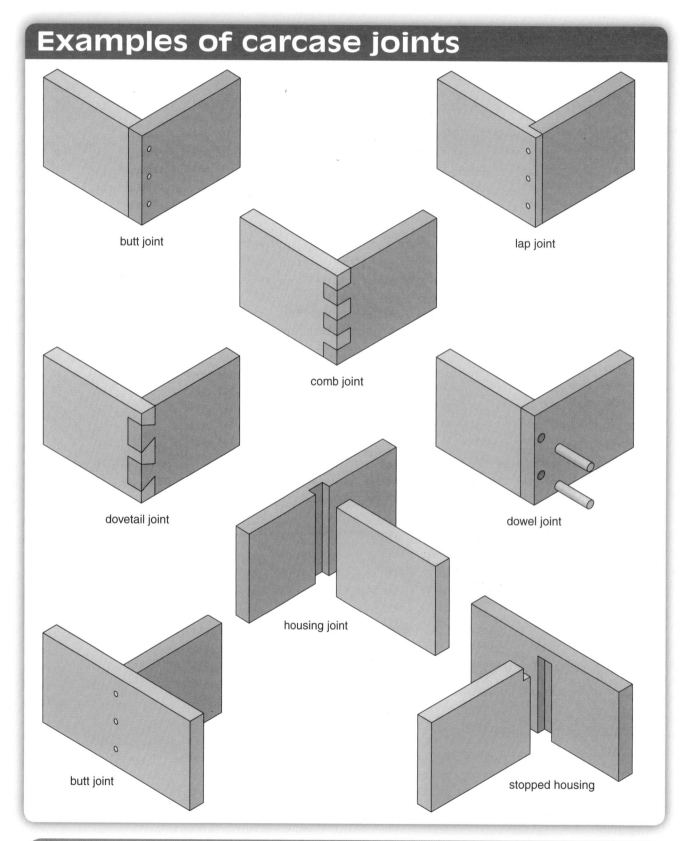

butt joint

lap joint

comb joint

dovetail joint

dowel joint

housing joint

butt joint

stopped housing

Quick Test

1. Where would a butt joint be used?

Answer   1 A butt joint is commonly used for rough joinery work where the ends are sawn or machined square and fixed by nailing.

Rebated butt joint

Due to the rebated or lap construction, this joint is stronger than the common butt joint. It has the added advantage that almost all of the end grain is hidden.

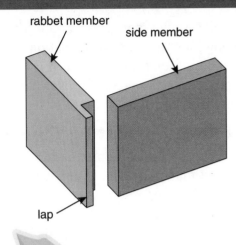

rabbet member
side member
lap

Marking out the joint

As with flat-frame joints, a practice joint may be made from a single length of material. After marking on the face side and face edge, square both ends on the disc sanding machine. Setting the marking gauge to the thickness of the material, gauge from one end across the face side and down each side. Set the marking gauge to about one quarter of the material thickness, and gauge a line across the end from the face side and along each edge to the shoulder-line. **Note:** although a marking gauge is commonly used for this procedure, a cutting gauge will give a cleaner mark.

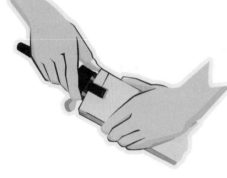

Marking the shoulder

Set a cutting gauge or a marking gauge to match the thickness of the side member, and gauge a shoulder-line parallel to the end on the back of the rebate member. Continue the shoulder-line across both edges to meet the gauge lines already scribed.

Cutting and assembly

With the joint fixed upright in the vice, carefully cut down to the waste side of the lap-line to the shoulder with a tenon saw. With the joint held face down on the sawing board, carefully saw down the shoulder-line to the waste side, and trim off with a block plane or bevel-edged chisel as necessary. Make sure that the rebate is clean and square to ensure a good fit. Assemble the joint with a thin spread of glue, and, with the assembly held in the vice, tap in say three pins in a dovetail pattern.

Top Tip
When sawing down to the waste side of a line, the teeth of the saw to one side should cut down the centre of the line.

Quick Test

1. What is meant by the term 'dovetail nailing'?

Answer   1 Dovetail nailing is where nails or pins are driven into a joint at an angle to each other in a dovetail pattern to add strength.

Rebated and grooved butt joint

This joint, sometimes called a bare-faced housing joint, is a stronger variation of the rebated butt joint, or lap joint. It is used mainly for machine-produced flat-pack furniture production.

Marking and cutting the groove

A practice joint may be made from a single length of material. After marking on the face side and face edge, square both ends on the disc sanding machine, and mark and square the mid-point all round. Setting the marking gauge to the wood thickness, mark on the inside edge of the groove from one end and return lightly down the edges. The outside line can now be gauged from the same end, making the groove no more than a quarter of the wood thickness.

Marking and cutting the rebate

Keeping the same setting, gauge along the other end from the face side and down both edges. With the marking gauge now set to one third the thickness of the material, gauge from the end along the face and down the edges. (This gauge setting can now be used to mark the bottom of the groove on both edges.) Form the rebate as before by sawing down the shoulder and chiselling to the line on the end. The groove can now be formed by sawing down and removing the waste by chiselling. (See p. 75, 'Through housing joint'.)

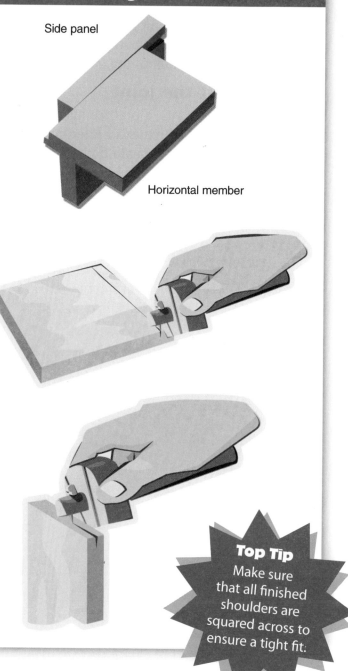

Side panel

Horizontal member

Top Tip
Make sure that all finished shoulders are squared across to ensure a tight fit.

Quick Test

1. What are the main features of the rebated and grooved butt joint?

Answer   1 The feather and groove are hidden, and the joint has added strength.

Mitred joint with slip-feather

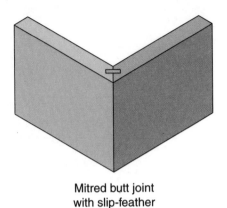

Mitred butt joint
with slip-feather

Top Tip
It is always better to cut the grooves slightly deeper to allow for expansion of the feather.

Top Tip
Make the slip-feather slightly smaller than the groove to allow for the glue.

Preparing the joint

The mitres are cut in the conventional manner. Slip-feathers are cut and planed to size (about 10 mm by 6 mm thick). Mark on the face side and face edge on all parts. The slip-feather grooves are marked by setting the marking pins of the mortice gauge to 3 mm and centring them on the wood thickness. Gauge on the grooves from the face side on each sawn mitre surface, and gauge on the groove depth on all four edges.

Care should be taken when marking on the slip-feather positions so that the grooves do not weaken the joint.

Holding each part in the vice, cut out the feather grooves with a 6 mm mortice chisel and clean out the bottom.

The joint can be glued and the slip-feathers inserted while the joint is held firmly in a mitre clamp. Wipe off surplus glue. Flush off top and bottom edges when glue is set.

Quick Test

1. What is the main advantage of this joint?

Answer **1** It forms a strong joint, and the end-wood cannot be seen.

The comb joint

The comb joint, sometimes called the box joint, is described here as a hand-made process, but the joint is produced commonly for high-quality box or carcase construction.

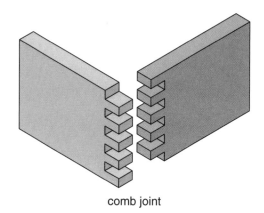

comb joint

Scribing the shoulder-lines

Square the ends of both components on the disc sanding machine. Set a cutting gauge or a marking gauge to the thickness of the wood, and lightly gauge a line from the end across the width and down each side of both ends, as shown.

Setting out the comb

With one part held upright in the vice, set out a number of equal divisions across the width of the member, and square these marks across the end and down each face to the shoulder-lines. Repeat the process on the other part, and make sure that they match with both face edges facing the same way. Note that one part will have pins at each end, and the matching half will have gaps to house them. Carefully mark out the waste wood on each part.

Cutting out the comb

With one part held vertically in the vice, saw down vertically to the waste side of each tooth-line to the shoulder-line. Cut out the waste wood between the teeth with a coping saw, being careful not to cut below the shoulder-line. Slice chisel neatly down to the shoulder-line on a chiselling board. Repeat the process for the other matching part.

Fitting the joint

Carefully fit the two halves of the joint together by hand to check the fit, and pare down any parts that are causing the joint to be too tight.

Top Tip

A quick method when forming a box is to pin two opposite sides together, mark and cut the joints together, then separate them and mark on the appropriate corners.

Quick Test

1. Why is this joint popular in decorative boxes?

Answers 1 Because of its simple form – it can be mass-produced cheaply using machines.

Through housing joint

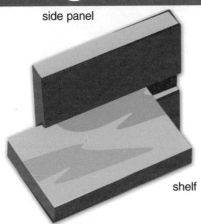

side panel

shelf

The through housing joint is relatively simple to make but shows on the front and back edges of side panels, and for this reason it is used mainly in cabinet work with shelves and face-fitted doors that hide the joint.

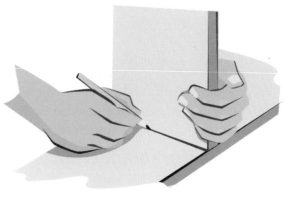

Marking out the joint

As before, a practice joint may be made from a single length of material. After marking on the face side and face edge, square both ends on the disc sanding machine, and mark and square the mid-point all round. Using a scrap piece of the same material, mark the position of the housing in the centre of one half. With a pencil or marking knife and try square, square these lines across and down both edges. Now set the marking gauge to the depth of the housing, which should be no more than a quarter of the thickness. Gauge on both edges from the face side between the housing-lines.

> **Top Tip**
> Keep both hands behind the cutting edge of the chisel during these processes.

Cutting the housing

Carefully saw down the waste side of the housing to the bottom gauge-lines. Remove the waste in the four stages described on pages 9 and 36. After parting off the two halves, fit the joint, paring the 'shelf' part with a smoothing plane if necessary.

> **Top Tip**
> If you have used a marking knife to mark the housing edges, make a small vee to the waste side of the line to start the tenon saw.

Quick Test

1. What is the main disadvantage of using this joint in, for example, a cabinet shelf?

Answer 1 The joint will show on the front edge.

Through multiple dovetail joint

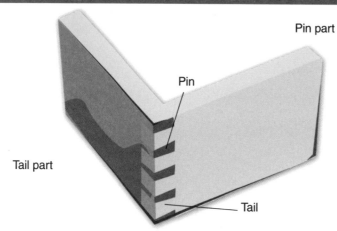

Pin part

Pin

Tail part

Tail

This is one of the most efficient joints for constructing carcase boxes, such as drawers. It is also one of the more difficult joints to cut and fit. The two parts of the joint, the pins and the tails, are visible on both sides of a corner and can be very attractive if well formed.

Marking the shoulder-lines

A practice joint may be made from a single length of material. After marking on the face side and face edge, square both ends on the disc sanding machine and mark and square the mid-point all round. With the marking gauge set to the thickness of the material, lightly gauge the shoulder-lines from each end all round the wood.

Spacing the tails

Fitting the material vertically in the vice with the face side towards you, measure and mark 6 mm from each edge and square across the end. Next, divide the space between into say 5 equal spaces, and measure 3 mm each side of these lines and square them across the end. Laying the wood flat on the bench, draw the sloping lines on the face side with a sliding bevel or **dovetail template** as shown.

Cutting the tails

With the workpiece held at an angle in the vice, saw down to the waste side of each tail, reversing the angle to complete the other side, as shown.

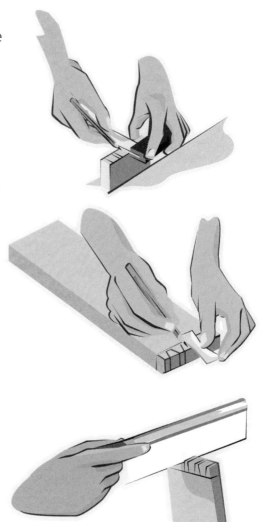

Removing the waste and cutting the shoulders

Saw down the outside corners with the workpiece held horizontally in the vice to remove the outside waste. With the workpiece now held vertically in the vice, the waste between the tails can be removed with a coping saw.

Lying the workpiece flat on the bench on top of a cutting board, the shoulders can be trimmed to the gauge-line by paring vertically from both sides with a bevel-edged chisel.

Marking the pins

After parting off the two halves, hold the pin half vertically in the vice with the machined end up. Now place the formed tails exactly over the end, and, holding the assembly square, draw round the tails with a sharp pencil to mark the pins. With a try square, draw these marks down both faces to the shoulder-line.

Cutting the pins

After carefully marking the waste wood between the pins, this can be removed with the coping saw as before, and pared down to the shoulder-line from both sides. The joint is assembled by holding the part with the pins vertically in the vice and gently tapping in the tails with a pin hammer and protective block. Careful paring will ease any parts that are too tight.

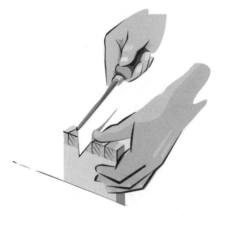

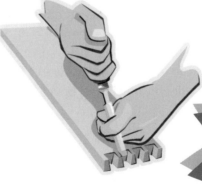

Top Tip
Check with a try square to see if the shoulder-lines are straight and square.

Top Tip
When marking the pins, coat the end of the vertical piece with chalk so that marked lines will stand out clearly.

Quick Test

1. Why is it important to line up the dovetail shoulders?

Answer 1 Because, if they are not in a perfectly straight line, gaps will show on the finished work.

Lapped multiple dovetail joint

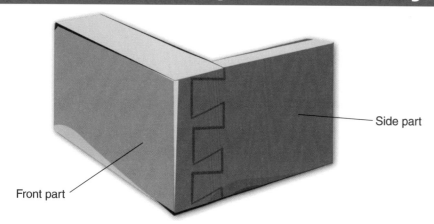

Side part

Front part

This is a joint that is universally used for making cabinet drawers, as one side of the joint is hidden. Usually, the part that has the pins is thicker to allow for the lap.

Marking the shoulder-lines

For this practice joint, two lengths of different thicknesses are required, one thinner part to represent the side of say a drawer, and a thicker part to represent the drawer front. The front part should be at least 5 mm thicker than the side part. Say the joint is to have four tails. After marking on the face side and face edge on both parts, square both ends of each on the disc sanding machine. With the marking gauge set to the thickness of the material, lightly gauge the shoulder-lines from the end, all round the side part and across the back face and on the edges of the front part. Keeping the same setting, gauge across the end of the front part from the back face.

Spacing the tails

Fitting the material vertically in the vice with the face side towards you, measure and mark 6 mm from each edge, and square across the end. Next, divide the space between into say five equal spaces, and measure 3 mm each side of these lines and square them across the end. Laying the wood flat on the bench, draw the sloping lines on the face side with a sliding bevel or **dovetail template** as with the through dovetail joint.

Cutting the tails

With the workpiece held at an angle in the vice, saw down to the waste side of each tail, reversing the angle to complete the other side, as shown.

Lapped dovetail joint

Removing the waste and cutting the shoulders

Saw down the outside corners with the workpiece held horizontally in the vice to remove the outside waste. With the workpiece now held vertically in the vice, the waste between the tails can be removed with a coping saw.

Lying the workpiece flat on the bench on top of a cutting board, the shoulders can be trimmed to the gauge-line by paring vertically from both sides with a bevel-edged chisel.

Marking the pins

Hold the front part vertically in the vice with the lap facing towards you. Now place the formed tails exactly over the end, only this time line the tail ends up with the lap line, and, holding the assembly square, draw round the tails with a sharp pencil to mark the pins. With a try square, draw these marks down the inside face to the shoulder-line.

Cutting the pins

After carefully marking the waste wood, the waste can be removed by holding the part vertically in the vice and sawing down at an angle to the waste side of each pin. Care should be taken not to cut the lap or below the shoulder-line. With the part now flat on the bench, the waste can be carefully chopped out with a 4-mm bevel-edged chisel and pared down evenly to the shoulder-line. The joint is assembled by holding the front part vertically in the vice and gently tapping in the tails with a pin hammer and protective block. As before careful paring will ease any parts that are too tight.

Top Tip
Check with a try square to see if the shoulder lines are straight and square.

Top Tip
Use a 4-mm bevel edged chisel to clean out the corners between the pins.

Quick Test

1. What is the main advantage of the lapped dovetail joint?

Answer   1   The end grain is hidden by the lap, so it is ideal for making drawer fronts and so on.

Edge-to-edge joints

Tongue joint

Tongue

With the increasing scarcity and cost of timber, it is often more economical to form a carcase panel by jointing strip wood together. Careful selection of the boards to be joined is required if the panel is to remain flat and not twist.

Planing the edges

When preparing a number of boards to be glued together to form a panel, it is better first to match the edges in pairs. First, lay out the boards in the correct grain order and mark the meeting edges and the best faces. Clamp each pair of boards in the vice with the face sides together, and plane each pair of edges straight and square until the meeting edges of each board have been straightened. By this method, if the boards are planed as a pair, they will match even if they are not exactly square.

Checking for straight edges

It is very important that the edges are straight and true, especially if a rubbed joint is to be formed.

Matching edges

Although it is good practice to plane edges as square as possible, if the boards have been planed as a pair, they will fit together and form a flat surface even when the edges are not exactly square.

Clamping the boards

First set out the sash clamps, preferably on boards across the bench, and adjust them to the appropriate size for clamping. Place the boards on the clamps in order, with protective strips at the outside edges. Clamp up with alternate clamps to even the pressure, and examine the boards for open seams. When satisfied with the jointing, loosen the clamps and apply glue to each edge in turn, and clamp the final assembly as shown. Ensure that you do not over-tighten the clamps; and lay weights on top to prevent warping.

Top Tip
Try to have the grain on the face of the strips running in the same direction to help in the cleaning-off process.

Top Tip
When forming a panel using a number of boards, try to clamp them with alternate grain patterns so that the members may shrink evenly.

Quick Test

1. Name three forms of edge-to-edge jointing systems.

Answer 1 Tongue and groove 2. Butt 3. Slip-feather

Dowel corner joint

Dowel corner joint

The standard dowel jig used in school workshops today consists of drill guides for vertical drilling that are adjustable along slide rods by means of end screws. For a right-angled butt joint, the jig assembly is clamped to the end of the workpiece held vertically in the vice, and adjusted to the correct hole positions with the fixed head to the face edge as shown. The side fence on the jig is adjusted so that the holes are drilled in the centre of the wood thickness. A ring called a **collet** is fitted to the drill shank by means of a screw so that the holes are drilled to the same desired depth.

Drilling matching holes

When drilling matching holes on the other part of the joint, it is essential to keep the same settings. The jig is turned upside down and fitted to the inside face, again with the fixed end to the face edge and with the side fence hard against the end grain, and the holes drilled as shown.

Top Tip
To ensure that dowels enter the holes cleanly when clamping up, sand a taper on the ends of each pre-cut dowel.

Quick Test

1. Why is it important to fit a depth stop to the drill bit?

Answer   1   So that the drill does not penetrate through the wood where it would be seen on the finished joint.

Carcase project – cabinet

Preparations

The cutting list

The cutting list is the standard method of communicating your needs to the workshop technician, who will machine the material to the sizes you specify.

Headings in the cutting list

A typical cutting list is normally divided into six columns; part, quantity, material, length, breadth and thickness. Each part of the project of the same size and material is set out under the 'part' heading. The quantity required of each part is entered under the 'quantity' heading. The material to be used for each part is stated under the 'material' heading. The length, breadth, and thickness are entered under the respective dimension headings.

Top Tip

When setting out sizes in a cutting list, try to make section sizes slightly bigger to allow for cleaning off.

part	number	material	length	breadth	thickness
top	1	pine	350	250	19
base	1	pine	350	250	19
ends	2	pine	500	250	19
shelf	1	pine	350	200	19
plinth	1	pine	350	100	19
door rails	2	pine	350	60	22
door stiles	2	pine	550	60	22
door panel	2	ply	380	230	3

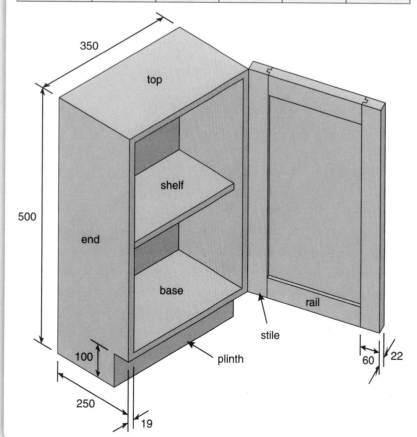

Marking out the wall-cabinet ends

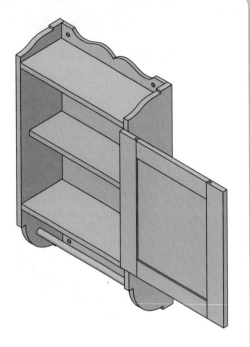

- Check the prepared material sizes against the working drawing, and plane to width as necessary.
- Mark on the face side and face edge on both parts.
- Cut ends to length, slightly oversize.
- Lightly square both ends to matching lengths.
- Lay both ends on the bench, face sides up and face edges touching. (The face edges will be the front edges and the face sides will be the inside.)
- Mark out the position of the top of the three shelves.
- Using a scrap of the same material, mark on the thickness of each shelf, and square across both faces using a pencil or marking knife.
- Set the marking gauge, and gauge on the distance in from the face edge for the stopped housings.
- Set the marking gauge to the depth of the housings, and lightly gauge both back edges from the face side. This will be your guide for running the rebate along the back edges of the ends.
- Mark out the shape of the curved ends with compasses or template.

Forming a rebate

- Set the rebate plane to the rebate width by adjusting the side fence so that the length of cutting iron exposed corresponds to the width of rebate to the gauge line.
- Set the depth stop of the rebate plane to the thickness of the back panel, adding 1 mm for dressing off.
- Clamp the workpiece horizontally in the vice, with the face side outwards, and the edge to be rebated uppermost.
- Start the rebate at the far end and work carefully back, taking longer and longer strokes, keeping the fence of the plane tight against the face side. If the shavings are rough, the cutting iron may need to be sharpened, or you are planing against the grain. Try taking a smaller cut with a sharp plane iron. (See p. 14, 'Rebate plane', and p. 42 on forming a rebate).

(See p. 14, 'Rebate plane', and p. 42 on forming a rebate).

Quick Test

Why is it necessary to **1.** Pair the ends of the carcase? **2.** Make the face edge the front?

Answers 1. So that the shelves and ends are perfectly in line. **2.** Because this is usually chosen as the best edge.

Shelves and back panel

Jointing the shelves

Stopped housing joint

The stopped housing joint is used in better-quality carcase construction where the shelf housing is stopped and does not show on the finished front edge.

Cutting the notch in the shelf

With the marking gauge still set to the depth of the housing, gauge in from the shelf-ends all round at the front edge. Next, again set the marking gauge to the size of the stopped housing end (usually about 15–20 mm) and gauge from the front edge at the ends of each shelf. Carefully cut out the notch to the waste side of the line and trim if necessary.

Stopped end

Forming the stopped housing

First, drill out the housing at the stopped end with a Forstner bit and form a shallow square trench to the required depth by morticing with a firmer chisel as shown. Saw down carefully to the waste side of the housing-lines, if necessary using the edge of a large try square set to the line as a guide. When the shoulders have been cut to the required depth, the waste can be removed by chipping out and paring with a bevel-edged chisel then finishing off with a pre-set router plane.

Top Tip
It is better to use two marking gauges: one for the depth and one for the stopped end.

Forming a curve

Mark on the curve details at top and bottom of the sides with either a pair of compasses and try square or a template. With the material clamped vertically in the vice, proceed to cut to the waste side of the line with smooth strokes, altering the blade angle if necessary as the cut proceeds. It is important not to hold the work too high in the vice, or the wood will vibrate causing a ragged saw-cut (see p. 21). Finish off the shaping with a cabinet file, and sand to produce a smooth curve with clean corners and edges.

The same process can be used to form the curves on the back panel, but extra care should be taken when sawing plywood so that the reverse edge does not become ragged. It is good practice to grip the ply panel well down in the vice so that the cut is firmly supported.

Assembling the carcase

Fit the shelves into the housings, paring out any tight parts. Carefully mark the shelf-ends to correspond with their housings. Lay out each component against the bench stop, and dress off any marks with a smoothing plane set for a fine cut. When cleaning off both sides of the shelves, take extra care to avoid planing the ends, or the joints will be slack. Finish off by sanding along the grain with medium sandpaper and a sanding cork.

The clamping process is straightforward if the following process is followed. Have all the sash clamps and protective blocks open and ready, with two clamps for every shelf member. Arrange the bottom clamps across the bench. Make sure that you have glue, a mallet and wet paper towels ready.

Top Tip
When forming the identical curves on both ends of the cabinet, align them face-to-face and pin them together with light gauge panel pins so that they can be cut and shaped together.

Top Tip
When marking corresponding joint parts, make the marks where they won't be cleaned off, i.e. on the ends and inside the housings.

Quick Test

1. Why is a cutting knife sometimes used to mark out joints such as housings?

Answer 1. Because the knife makes a more accurate cut that is easier to work to.

Carcase project – cabinet (cont.)

Lay out the components flat on the bench, face up and end-to-end with corresponding joints touching.

Begin by applying glue evenly to both parts of one joint at a time and tapping the shelves into their housings on one side panel. When all the shelves have been fitted to one side, place the remaining side over the top, and guide each shelf into its housing. Ensure at this stage that the backs of all the shelves are flush with the inside of the rebate.

Set the assembled carcase into the bottom clamps, making sure that the protective strips are in place. With each clamp in line with a shelf, tighten the clamps carefully to squeeze each joint tight. Place the remaining sash clamps over each shelf and repeat the tightening process. Carefully wipe off all surplus glue from the top and bottom of the carcase. Square the carcase using a try square and a squaring rod, or a steel rule to compare the diagonals. (See page 59, squaring a frame).

Top Tip
Remember that every run of glue not wiped off thoroughly will show as a mark through any varnish finish.

Fitting a back panel

After the glue is set, lay the carcase face down on the bench and ensure that the back edges of each shelf and the inside of the rebate are flush clean and straight. To fit the back panel, first plane one long edge straight while clamped in the vice. Then plane a short edge so that a perfectly square corner is formed. Mark these two edges on the panel. Fit the long edge into the carcase rebate and along the top marking on the width of the panel, pulling the carcase to the square panel if necessary, and draw a line. Plane down to the line carefully and try the panel for fit. This process is repeated to complete the panel height on the carcase. The planing and fitting process may have to be repeated several times, especially with larger panels. When a final comfortable fit is achieved, apply glue evenly to the edges of the shelves and the rebate, and secure the panel finally with evenly spaced panel pins.

1 squaring two edges

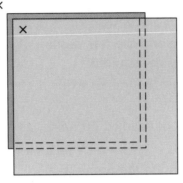

2 fitting and marking side edge

A back panel is shown fitted to a rebate on all sides with curve omitted

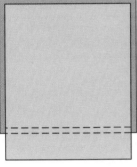

3 fitting and marking bottom edge

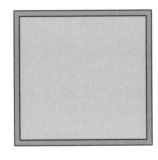

4 final fit

Finishing off

With the carcase clamped firmly in the vice or set against the bench stop, clean off both sides with the smoothing plane and finish off with sandpaper and a cork. Take the sharp corners off by lightly sanding, but do not round the edges.

Quick Test

1. Describe briefly the stages of fitting a cabinet back panel into a rebate.

Answers **1** Plane the long and short edges of the panel straight and square to each other. **2.** Fit the long edge into the rebate and mark off the panel width. **3.** Cut and plane to the line, fit the panel to the top and mark off the panel length. **4.** Cut and plane to the line, and fit panel.

Fitting a door to a carcase frame

Fitting a door inside a carcase frame

Fitting a door consisting of a flat frame into the opening of a carcase box requires a special procedure involving a number of stages.

- The first stage is to fit the hingeing side.
- Decide which face of the door is going to be on the outside, and mark the hingeing stile.
- Plane the edge of this stile, and plane its corresponding top edge square to it.
- Fit these two edges into the carcase to see if they fit along the hinge edge and the top. Some further planing and fitting may be required.
- Mark off the door width against the frame, scribe a line and plane down to that line.
- The height of the door should be marked off next. Plane down to the line drawn.

The door should now fit evenly inside the frame, but some final trimming may be required to produce even clearance all round. The traditional clearance for an internal door is the thickness of a two-pence piece.

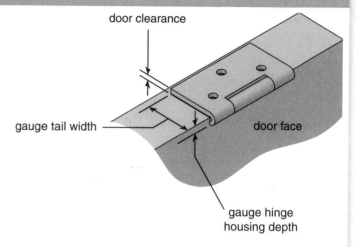

fitting edge butt hinges

Fitting the hinges

It is important to first identify the hingeing edge of the door. In this case, the hingeing edge of the door will be the outside corner, which will be matched to the inside corner of the carcase frame.

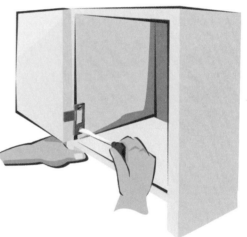

In this case, we are using brass butt hinges; but, whatever hinge is used, the centre-line of the **hinge ball** (the pin running through the centre of the hinge) should be in line with the hingeing corner of the door. With the door held in the vice with the hinge corner towards you, mark on the length of each hinge on the edge of the door, and square across and partway down the front face of the door. Set the marking gauge to the distance between the centre of the hinge **pin** and the **tail**. Gauge along the edge from the front of the door face, between the hinge lines. Next, set the marking gauge to the depth the hinge is to be sunk into the door edge (**the full thickness of the hinge ball minus the clearance**) and gauge on the front face from the door edge.

Carefully saw down at an angle to the waste side of the hinge lines and chip out the waste with a mallet and chisel, then fit and screw the hinge in place in the housing. When the hinges are fitted as shown and folded close, place a rule over the hinge to check the clearance. The amount of hinge projecting up should be no more than the door clearance.

Fitting a door to a carcase

Fit the door to the frame by holding the door in place with the hinges open, and mark each hinge position. Square these marks across inside the frame. Set the marking gauge to the distance from the front face of the door and the tail of the hinge when folded, leaving an additional 1 mm for clearance. Scribe gauge marks inside the frame between the hinge-lines. Carefully hold the door in position and screw-fix the hinges to the scribed marks.

Fitting a door inside a carcase frame using flush hinges

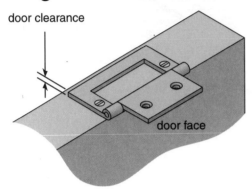

fitting flush hinges

This is a much simpler process, as the hinge when closed is the same as the door clearance, so there is no need to sink the hinge into the wood. It is merely a matter of marking the hinge position and screwing the hinge straight on to the door with the hinge ball tight against the door edge.

Mark the position of the hinges on the door frame, as before. After squaring the marks across, gauge on the distance from the front of the door, and gauge and scribe. Holding the door open, fix the hinges in place to the gauge-line.

Fitting a door to the face of the carcase using flush hinges

This is the simplest method of hingeing a door, as there is no need for fitting. The door is fitted to the front face of the carcase (known as face filling). The procedure is the same, only the hinge is fitted to the back of the door to the hingeing corner.

Top Tip

After fixing the hinges to the door, fit the door to the carcase with one screw in each hinge to try the fit – then you can see what adjustments need to be made.

Quick Test

1. When the door will not close properly, what two things could be wrong?

2. What can be done to correct these errors and allow the door to close properly?

Answer 1. The door is too large for the opening, or it could be 'hinge bound'. 2. If the door is too large, it has to be planed on the side or the end. If the door is 'hinge bound', the tail of the hinge needs to be sunk further into the carcase.

Making a simple drawer

For the purposes of this guide, we will consider making a drawer to fit into a carcase structure. The simplest form of drawer is constructed using butt-dowelled corners, fitted-on guide rails and a 'planted-on' drawer front. A ply bottom is fitted on strip fillets fixed to the underside of the drawer.

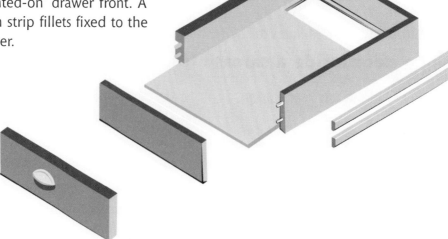

Drawer front

The drawer front is first fitted carefully to the drawer opening in the carcase. The second, or false front, is fitted with slightly more clearance; alternatively, the drawer front can be face-fitted on the carcase front.

The sides and back

Prepare the sides and back to the correct width for the opening. Cut the sides to length, about 40 mm shorter than the inside carcase depth. Pair the sides and machine both ends square. When cutting the back and false front to length, remember that the overall width of the drawer will be narrower than the drawer front to allow for the drawer guides at each side, i.e. the length of the back and false front will be the length of the drawer front plus twice the thickness of the drawer guides.

Top Tip
Make the drawer back narrower than the sides, and leave a space at the drawer's top edge to let air escape when closing.

Making the dowel joints

The sides are laid on the bench with the face sides up (the inside of the drawer) and the face edges towards you (the bottom of the drawer). (See p. 86 for assembling a carcase.) The dowels are dry-fitted to the corners as described on p. 81, using a dowel jig.

Fitting the fillets

After the dowel corner joints have been formed, the fillets can be fitted to the inside of the four drawer sides at the bottom edge (the face edge).

Assembling the drawer

The four corner dowelled joints can now be glued, fitted, clamped and squared. Carefully remove any surplus glue immediately. The ply drawer bottom is now fitted to the inside and glued and pinned to the fillets. The drawer guides can now be fitted as indicated.

Making a drawer using dovetails

The drawer front in this case is formed as part of the drawer carcase with no false front and is usually thicker to accommodate the lapped dovetail jointing (see pp. 78–9, 'Lapped multiple dovetail joint'). The two back corners are formed using standard through dovetails.

Making and fitting a drawer

After preparation, the sides and ends are laid on the bench with the face sides up (the inside of the drawer) and the face edge towards you (the bottom of the drawer). See page 85 for assembling a carcase.

Forming the joints

Lay out the prepared components on the bench as shown, and carefully mark where each joint is to be formed. Form the corner dovetails as detailed on pages 78 and 79.

Grooving the sides

Set the combination plane with a 3-mm cutter to the distance from the drawer bottom and a depth of approximately half the side thickness. With each side clamped to the bench against the bench stop, run a groove on each component. See running a groove, page 72.

Drawer fitting

First the drawer runners, or guides, are fitted in place inside the carcase to correspond with those fixed to the drawer in the same manner as before. Then fit the drawer into the guides, and fix a piece of ply inside the carcase under the top rail so that the drawer stops with the drawer front flush with the face of the carcase.

Many different types of drawer guides are now available commercially, some with nylon guides, or high-quality versions with ball bearings set into sealed channels to provide a perfectly smooth drawer operation.

Top Tip
Ensure that the groove is covered by the tail of the side dovetails.

Top Tip
A good way to ease a drawer that is sticking is to rub a candle along the drawer guides.

Quick Test

1. Why is the back of a drawer narrower than the sides and front?

Answer 1 To let the air escape when shutting the drawer.

Unit 3 – Machining and Finishing

What you will learn

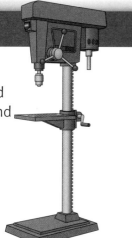

Fixed machine tools

In this unit, you will learn to set up and use a range of common fixed machine tools. You will also learn about the safe working practices and health and safety rules associated with fixed machine tools.

The range of fixed machine tools includes the vertical drill, woodworking lathe (faceplate turning and between centres), belt and disc sanding machine and bench grinder (grinding chisels). You will learn, and be tested on, machining to specific pre-determined tolerances in the correct sequence.

Portable power tools

You will learn how to set up and use a range of common portable power tools, using the appropriate work methods, in accordance with health and safety regulations and to specific pre-determined tolerances.

The range of portable power tools includes the portable power drill, jig-saw, various sanders and power screwdrivers.

Finishing techniques

You will learn to use surface finishing techniques on timber products and will be tested on both your choice of appropriate finishing materials and the process. The preparation of finishing materials in accordance with the manufacturer's instructions is also part of the learning process.

Surface preparation and application of finishes

Surface preparations will include planing, scraping, sanding, stopping and filling. You will be taught, and be tested on, the correct method of applying a range of surface finishes. These finishes will include varnish and oil- and water-based paints, including undercoats. All finishes will be applied by brush and will consist of two coats.

Machining-and-finishing project

The machining-and-finishing evidence produced will be in the form of a project that you will mark out and machine within specified tolerances from a working drawing that will be supplied. You will be assessed on the various processes involved, the terminology used, and how you perform these tasks. There will be written tests at appropriate stages on your knowledge and understanding of machines, their parts, and how to set up in preparation for a particular process with due regard for safety.

Top Tip
This is a good time to start your machine log. Enter details of your experience of each machine tool.

Wood-turning

Wood-turning is very popular, and skills evidence in the finished product can be easily measured. You must work to dimensions and to a pre-determined tolerance. For example, a piece of turnery may be tested on its length and two or three diameters taken from the working drawing.

Examples of projects

Wine table

Table lamp

Quick Test

1. Name the fundamental safety check on any machine before you start.

Answer   1   Make sure the power is switched off before setting up the machine.

Fixed machine tools

Wood-turning lathe

The wood-turning lathe is a fixed machine tool used for converting square section wood into spindle or circular form and for turning to a pre-determined shape using special chisels and gouges. The wood-turning lathe generally consists of four main parts – the bed, the headstock, the tailstock and the tool rest. The bed is the main part of the machine, and every other part is attached to it, as shown below.

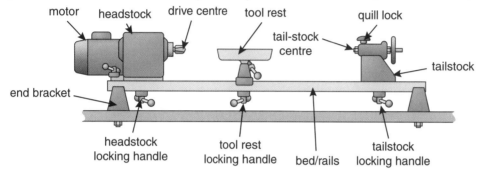

The headstock

This is the driving part of the machine, housing the spindle and drive centre powered by the motor. The drive spindle projects through to the outer end of the headstock, where a faceplate can be attached for turning large-diameter work such as bowls. Normally in school and college workshops, the headstock is fixed and not adjustable.

The tailstock

The tailstock can be adjusted to the length of the turnery workpiece by sliding it along the bed of the lathe and locking by means of a quick-lock lever located under the bed.

The tool rest

As the name suggests, the tool rest can be height-adjusted and can also line up the chisel with the turnery. Additionally, a tool rest can be fitted for faceplate turning.

Preparing the blank for turning

Before starting to turn a piece of square timber on the lathe, it must first be cut to a length about 70 mm longer than the finished product. Both ends must be centred by joining the diagonals. On one end, saw-cuts are made, so that the drive-centre spurs can be housed. Holes are drilled at each end to ease the fitting of the workpiece between the centres. Scribe the biggest circle possible on each end, and, placing the blank in the vice, plane each corner down to the circle to form an octagonal bar. A spokeshave can also be used for this process.

Setting up for basic turning

Ensure that the mains power to the machine is switched off. After moving the tailstock clear, enter the blank at the saw-cut end into the drive centre and gently tap home with a mallet. Some lubricant, such as tallow, is applied to the other end of the blank. Move the tailstock close until the tailstock centre enters the hole at the other end of the blank, and tighten the tailstock. Adjust the handwheel until the blank is firmly fixed between the two centres. Adjust the tool rest so that it is parallel and just clear of the workpiece when it is turned by hand. The top edge of the tool rest should be about 15 mm below the centre-line of the lathe centres in order to allow for the turning tool.

Top Tip Bind the ends of the turnery blank with masking tape to prevent splitting.

Forming the shape

Before switching on the power to the machine, make sure that the workpiece can be turned freely by hand without fouling the tool rest and that the workpiece is secure between the centres. Switch on the power and the dust extractor, and then start the machine. Lathe tools are produced in three basic types – gouges, scrapers and special tools. The lathe tool should be held at a slight angle downwards and firmly down on the tool rest.

Top Tip
If the gouge is tilted slightly to the side, the cuttings will fly to the side and not over the operator.

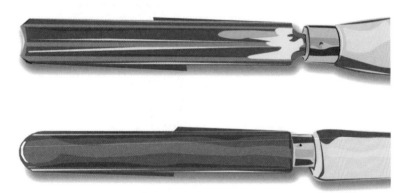

Roughing gouges

A roughing gouge is used first to turn the workpiece from its octagonal shape into a cylinder shape. It is ground and sharpened on the bevelled underside only, so that a sharp cutting burr is formed on the inside.

Spindle or fingertip gouges

These gouges, so called because their rounded point resembles a fingertip, are shaped to make delicate shapes and to get inside curves that a roughing gouge could not access.

Quick Test

1. Gouges are sharpened only on the bevelled underside. Explain the reason for this.

Answer   1 The sharp burr formed on the top edge of the chisel helps in the cutting process, and the edge stays sharp longer.

Using a gouge

The secret of using a gouge when wood-turning is to hold the tool at the correct angle. To do this, start by holding the handle down with the tool shank firmly on the tool rest and the bevel on the underside of the chisel, against the turnery. Raise the handle of the gouge until you see it cutting smoothly. Stop the machine occasionally to check the roundness and check shape and diameters with pre-set outside callipers.

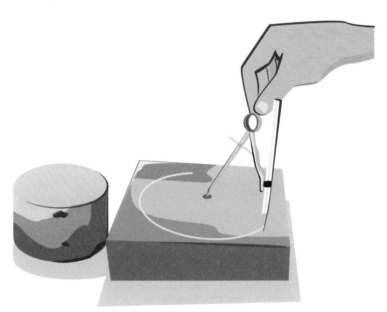

Faceplate turning

Faceplate turning is used to turn large-diameter items such as bowls and bases for lamps. The workpiece blank should be prepared as before and then screwed centrally on to a faceplate, which is attached to the outside end of the headstock in most lathes. The tool rest should then be adjusted in place. **Remember to go through all the safety checks before switching on the lathe**.

Top Tip
When fitting a blank for bowl-turning to the face-plate, ensure that fixing screws do not penetrate too deeply.

Quick Test

1. Name four safety checks carried out before using a wood-turning lathe.

2. Name the main parts of the lathe.

3. Explain the shape and purpose of **a)** a roughing gouge, **b)** a scraper.

Answers 1. Check that the main power is switched off; set up the turnery blank between the centres; set the tool rest in position to the correct height and clearance; turn the workpiece by hand to ensure correct clearance. **2.** Bed, headstock, tailstock, tool rest. **3 a)** A roughing gouge has a hollow shape with either a square or a rounded end and is used for roughing work down to cylinder form. **b)** A scraper has a square or a round or a skewed end and is used to scrape a surface smooth.

Mortice machine

morticing bit

handle

clamp

movable bed

handwheel

Machine morticing

Most teaching workshops have a purpose-made mortice machine that consists of a movable bed where the workpiece is clamped and a square hole of the required size is drilled to the required depth in the workpiece.

Morticing bits

The square hole drilled to form the mortice is produced by a bit attached to the head of the machine. The mortice bit consists of an auger bit that rotates inside a square-edged chisel. The bit cuts a round hole, and the chisel punches it square. The auger is fitted into the chuck, and the bit is clamped into the quill frame on the machine.

Setting up for morticing

Most mortice machines have a fixed fence fitted to the movable bed of the machine. After ensuring that the power to the machine is switched off, clamp the workpiece against the fence and down on the bed, with the mortice to be cut centrally in the bed. By pulling down on the handle, the bit will be lowered on to the workpiece, and by adjusting the front handwheel the bit is aligned with the mortice gauge-lines. It may be necessary to fit packing under the workpiece to raise it higher.

Top Tip
When morticing, always place the face side of the workpiece against the fence.

Depth stop

With the machine still isolated from its power, lower the morticing bit until it is resting on the top edge of the workpiece. Adjust the depth stop to the depth you require. In the case of a through mortice, set the stop to just over half the material width, and tighten the locking lever.

Cutting the mortice

It may be that the machine will still be set up for the last person who used it – so don't assume that the settings will be exactly the same for you. Go through the safety checks first, and then make sure that the chisel bit comes down exactly between your mortice gauge-lines. Always assume that you will have to do your own set-up checks. Pulling down the lever to cut the mortice will require some effort, depending on the hardness of the wood – but don't pull down too hard, or the bit will burn in the mortice and will be difficult to remove when the handle is raised. Starting at one end of the mortice, steadily progress one slot at a time towards the other end, finishing precisely on the mortice-line.

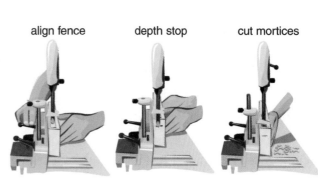

align fence   depth stop   cut mortices

Quick Test

1. Name four main parts of the mortice machine, and explain their function.

Pedestal drilling machine

The drilling machine

This machine is sometimes called a pillar drill, or drill press, and is the most versatile and commonly used machine in the teaching workshop. It consists of five main parts: the head, the column, the base, the table and the chuck.

The head

The head houses the gearing, motor, power switch, feed handle and chuck.

The column

The column is the main pillar that holds the parts of the machine together and houses a toothed rack for moving the table to different heights.

The base

The base is usually made of cast steel and gives the drilling machine stability. The base is bolted to the floor for additional support.

The table

The table has a top surface that is machined true and can be moved up and down by a handle that drives a cogwheel on the toothed rack of the column.

The chuck

This is the business part of the drilling machine and can be opened or closed by means of a chuck key to receive drill bits. A clear plastic folding guard is fitted round the chuck for the added safety of the operator.

Drilling operation

Before starting any drilling operation, a number of safety checks must be carried out. With the machine isolated from its power, insert the drill in the chuck and tighten securely with the chuck key. **Safety note: Always remove the chuck key from the chuck before start-up.**

Holding the workpiece

If the workpiece to be drilled is small, it should be clamped in a machine vice or clamped to the machine table.

Diagram labels: cover conceals v-belt and pulleys, power switch, motor, quill, feed handle, chuck, table-height adjustment handle, rack-and-pinion system, table, column, base

Top Tip
Safety goggles should be worn during machining operations, and loose clothing and ties kept clear, long hair should be tied back. See safety rules pages 6 and 7.

Top Tip
Always ensure that the table is adjusted to a suitable height for lowering the drill on to the work.

Quick Test

1. Name four safety checks carried out before using the drilling machine.

Answers 1 Check that the machine is switched off. **2.** Check that the drill is fitted properly in the chuck. **3.** Check that the chuck key is removed from the chuck. **4.** Check that the workpiece is held securely.

Drum sanders

The drum sander

A drum sander, as the name implies, is a round cylinder of rubber that is tightened inside a sanding sleeve. The shank of the drum sander fits into a standard machine chuck. These tools are supplied in various lengths and diameters and are very useful for finishing both internal and external curved work. As with all machine work, eye protection must be worn.

Drum sanders in a portable drill

A drum sander fitted to a portable drill is very useful for sanding curves on a cabinet structure where a fixed machine cannot be used. Great care should be taken to move the drill in the opposite direction to the spinning drum while keeping the drum parallel to the surface to be finished. If you move the tool in the direction the drum is spinning, it tends to grab and run along the work out of control. This machine should be used only under close supervision.

Drum sanders in a pedestal drilling machine

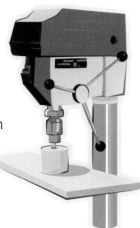

The main difference between using a drum sander in a fixed machine and using it in a portable drill is that the workpiece is presented to the spinning drum, and both hands are on the workpiece. Here again, it is important to move the workpiece in the opposite direction to the drum and to work slowly and steadily along the curve.

On the wood-turning lathe

There are drum sanders that can be fitted to the lathe. The drum has a pin on one end to fit into the lathe's tailstock, and crossed notches on the drive end to fit a standard drive centre on the headstock. Some versions have an inflatable core that fits inside the sanding sleeve, and the stiffness of the drum can be modified by the amount of air you pump into the core.

Top Tip
To ensure even wear on the drum, drill a large-diameter hole in a piece of blockboard so that the drum can be raised and lowered.

Quick Test

1. Why is it important to keep the movement between the drum and the workpiece?

Answer 1 So that the curve is even and that no burning occurs.

Belt-disc sanding machines and fixed jig-saws

Sanding machines

Sanding machines are found in various forms, such as belt sanders, horizontal and vertical, disc sanders, and combination machines with both systems. All surface abrasive machines, although relatively safe to use, should be operated with care, and the workpiece should be placed against the guide and presented gently to the sanding surface. If greater pressure is exerted, the surface being sanded will start to burn.

Top Tip

When using the sanding disc, always use the downward rotating side. Apply slow, even pressure across the sanding surface of both belt and disc.

Fixed jig-saw machine

This machine is found in two versions – bench-mounted or free-standing. A fixed jig-saw machine is relatively safe and easy to use, but can generally only be used for forming curves in light material. If too much pressure is used, the blade may break, so a very careful approach is required.

Quick Test

1. Name the first health-and-safety check before using a dust-emitting machine.

Answer 1 Check that the dust-extractor system is switched on.

Portable power tools

Portable power screwdriver

The portable power screwdriver has become very popular in school and college workshops. It is relatively safe to use and very versatile, with quick-change heads for both cross-head and slot-head applications of various sizes. Specially adapted drill bits can also be fitted for drilling small pilot holes for screws.

Type and description

This is a very versatile and useful tool, with a number of octagonal-shaped tool-bits that fit into a standard housing in the tool. Most types have an angled body for driving screws near a corner; and cordless rechargeable heavy-duty versions are now in common use.

Operation

The portable screwdriver is a simple machine to use with a forward, reverse and neutral control button. The bits can be quickly changed to suit a number of screwdriving situations.

For heavier work, and as an alternative, screwdriver bits can be fitted into modern power drills with variable speeds.

Top Tip
When using a power screwdriver, always hold the tool so that the bit enters the screw head at right angles.

Top Tip
Before using a portable screwdriver, make sure that the screwdriver bit is the correct size for the screw head.

Quick Test

1. Why is it so important to attach a dust extractor to dust-emitting machine tools?

Answer   1 Because certain dust particles are so fine that they could cause lung damage over a long period of time.

Portable jig-saws

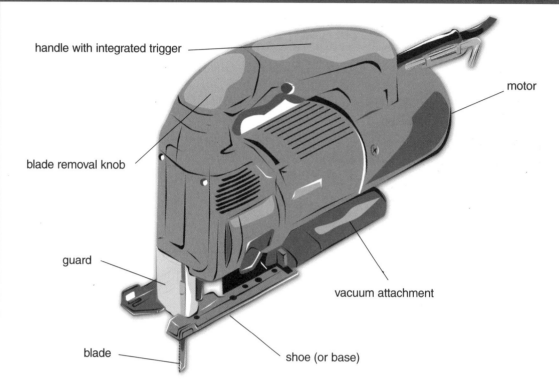

handle with integrated trigger

motor

blade removal knob

guard

vacuum attachment

blade

shoe (or base)

Types and description

The jig-saw, or sabre saw as it is sometimes called, comes in two basic versions: standard and orbital. The standard jig-saw's blade simply moves vertically up and down, while the orbital jig-saw is much more robust and its blade cuts through the wood with a rotating action at variable speeds. It is now compulsory to have a dust-bag attached to an orbital jig-saw. Rechargeable cordless versions are now widely in use in school workshops. A removable clear plastic chip-guard is now a common feature.

Operation

The set-up checks and use must be planned and carried out before making a cut. Ensure that the workpiece is securely clamped or held and that there is clear space under the area to be cut. Check that the guard is in place and an empty dust-bag connected, and that the power cable is clear. Make a slow and steady cut, ensuring that you can see the line at all times. If you have to stop the machine, extract the blade carefully and re-enter at the end of the cut.

Top Tip
When using corded portable power tools, it is a good idea to drape the power cable over the opposite shoulder, as this ensures that it is always clear of the blade.

Quick Test

1. Name the four main parts of the portable jig-saw.

2. What are the main safety checks when using a portable jig-saw with mains power cord?

Answers 1. The blade, the shoe or base, and the on/off trigger. **2.** Check that the blade is fitted properly, then check that the workpiece is held firmly and that the blade will be clear of obstructions.

Portable sanding machines

Types and description

The most common power sander is the orbital sander, which makes a circular motion of the baseplate on the surface when the trigger is pressed. A number of portable sanders are produced for special purposes: the palm-grip sander is used for light work; the delta sander, with its triangular shape, is useful for sanding into corners. Rechargeable cordless versions are now in common use. All portable sanders should be used with a dust-extraction bag attached.

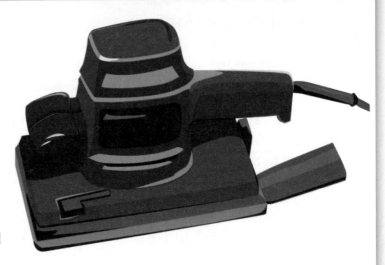

Orbital sander operation

Specially-cut strips of graded sandpaper are available to fit onto the baseplate, based on a standard sheet (see abrasives pages 108 and 109). To avoid clogging, perforated sandpaper strips can be used. Orbital sanders should be used with a steady, even pressure, as excessive force leads to overheating and clogging of the sandpaper sheet. Keep the machine moving evenly back and forth along the grain, and try not to move across the grain, as this can leave circular marking.

Portable belt sanders

The portable belt sander is becoming very popular because of its versatility and its ability to sand both internal and external curves. Care should be taken, however, to sand in the opposite direction to the belt rotation, as with drum sanders.

Top Tip
When using a portable sander, stop frequently and knock the dust from the baseplate and sandpaper. This will make the sandpaper last longer.

Quick Test

1. What is the meaning of the word orbital?

2. Why is this function important in sanding wood?

Answers 1. Orbital means that the sanding action is circular. 2. The sanding base goes round in very tight circles so that cross-grain scratches are avoided at corners when sanding an object such as a flat frame, which has different grain directions.

Portable power drills

Types and description

Mains-powered portable drills are used universally and can perform a number of tasks such as screwdriving, or can be adapted for lathe work or clamped into a vertical drilling frame. Cordless rechargeable portable drills are now very common and are supplied in a wide variety of makes, with speed and hammer selection to suit a range of drilling operations in wood, metal and masonry.

depth stop — hammer-action switch — speed selection — keyless chuck — reverse-action switch — variable-speed trigger — lock button — CRM-114

The main parts

Perhaps the most important part of the power drill is the chuck. This is similar to the standard Jacobs chuck found on pillar drilling machines, which has an outer toothed ring where a special chuck key is inserted to open the chuck jaws. Many modern power drills are fitted with keyless chucks that tighten the drill bit by holding a collar behind the chuck while the drill is moving slowly. A depth stop in the form of an adjustable rod, and a front handle for additional control, are also very useful features.

Operation

In order to operate a power drill safely and accurately, a number of points must be observed. When drilling either horizontally or vertically, care should be taken to keep the drill bit at right angles to the surface being drilled. Extra pressure can be applied by the shoulder on the hand holding the pistol grip. Always keep the drill bit tightly fixed in the chuck. Ties, loose clothing and long hair should be kept well back from the chuck area – and always keep the drill chuck away from your body. Wait until the drill has stopped before putting it down safely.

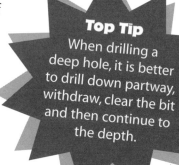

Top Tip
When drilling a deep hole, it is better to drill down partway, withdraw, clear the bit and then continue to the depth.

Quick Test

1. Why is it very important when operating a power drill to keep ties, long hair and loose clothing away from the chuck area?

Answer 1 Because these items could become entangled with the rotating chuck, resulting in injury.

Portable biscuit jointer

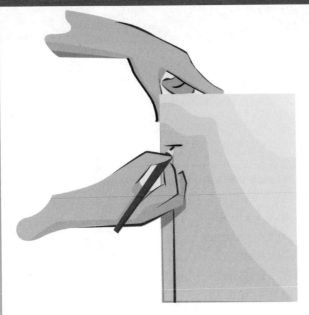

Top Tip

It is very important to clamp the workpiece securely and hold the machine firmly with both hands before the cutting blade enters the wood.

Types and description

A biscuit jointing machine has become a very useful addition to the teaching workshop. The system involves cutting a matching slot on the face of two pieces of wood to be joined and inserting a 'dovetail-shaped' piece of wood called a biscuit. The biscuit is made of hardwood with a very low moisture content, so that when water-based glue is applied it swells and forms a tight joint.

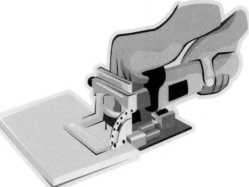

Operation

To form a simple butt joint between two flat pieces of wood of equal thickness, simply place them together and mark across the joining edge the number of fixings required, as shown above. Clamp one piece flat on the bench, and, presenting the jointer square to the edge with its reference pointer lined up to the reference mark, gently squeeze the trigger – and the slot is cut.

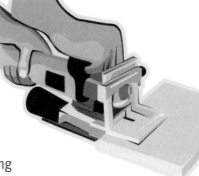

Cut the slot in the other half of the joint in exactly the same manner, paying particular attention to lining up the marks perfectly. After cleaning out any dust from the slots, the joint can be formed by applying glue to the meeting edges, clamping in the usual manner then gluing and tapping in the biscuits with a pin hammer.

Quick Test

1. What are the most important safety rules when using a portable biscuit jointer?

Answer 1 Keep everything clamped tightly, and keep both hands on the machine.

Machined projects

Wine table

Description

This wine-table project comprises a shaped top with supporting rails, turned central spindle and shaped feet, all substantially manufactured using fixed and portable power tools.

Central spindle

Before the central spindle is turned on the lathe, the square section can be part-jointed at the top and bottom ends to receive the feet and top supports. It has been found from experience that instead of stub mortice-and-tenon joints, the feet are jointed more securely using a dovetail housing where the feet can be slotted in from the end. So, before turning, the joints can be partly cut using the mortice machine. The blank is prepared and fitted into the turning lathe in the manner described on page 76, and turned to the required shape and tolerances. When the turning is complete and parted off, the dovetail housings can be cut from the mortices to the required size and cleaned out.

Forming the curved feet

A template can be used to mark out the feet, which can then be cut with the jig-saw and spokeshaved, filed and sanded to the shape. The dovetails can now be formed and fitted to the spindle housings.

Forming the top

The supports for the top can be formed in two pieces, shaped and jointed with a cross-halving joint and housed into slots in the top of the spindle.

The shape of the top can be formed by first jointing several pieces of appropriate wood together. Either plain butt or slip-feather joints may be used. When set, the shape of the top can be marked out and cut with the jig-saw. A hand-run moulding or simple chamfer may be added, or the technician may run a machine moulding to produce the desired edge finish.

Final assembly

First, fit and glue the feet to the spindle and then the top supports, making sure to check for alignment and square. The top can be fixed using screws inserted through pre-bored holes in the supports.

Table lamp

Description

This table-lamp project comprises a turned central spindle and turned base, both manufactured using the wood-turning lathe.

Forming the spindle

The spindle is turned from a prepared blank as described on page 94. It is better to form a ply half-profile first and work to the tolerances of the shape, instead of just seeing how it turns out. A hole is driven through the centre of the spindle with an **extension auger bit** inserted through the **hollow tailstock centre**. Final finishing can now be carried out on the lathe.

Forming the base

The base can be turned on the baseplate of the turning lathe, as described on page 95. A scribed and cut circular wood disc is first secured to the baseplate and fitted to the machine with the tool rest correctly fitted (as described on p. 96). The base is turned to a pre-determined shape and worked to within stated tolerances. Final finishing can now be carried out on the lathe.

Final assembly

A hole is drilled through the edge of the base and connected to one drilled through the base centre. Before the spindle is fitted to the base, the electrical flex and lamp-holder can be inserted.

Top Tip
Ensure that the screws fixing the workpiece to the base-plate are not too long so that they do not penetrate into the shape to be cut.

Quick Test

1. Name the stages of preparing a blank for turning.

Answers 1. Cut to appropriate length. **2.** Centre both ends by diagonals. **3.** Drill centre holes in each end. **4.** Do saw-cuts and 'V' cuts to one end. **5.** Plane or spokeshave the corners to an octagonal shape. Tape the ends to prevent splitting.

Surface finishing

Finishing materials

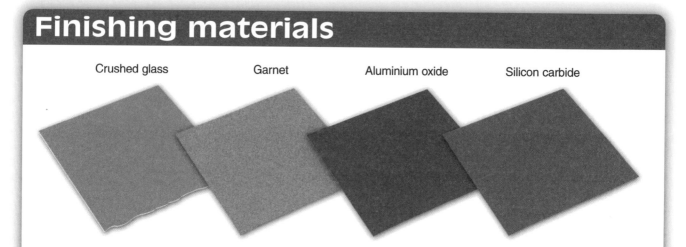

Crushed glass　　　Garnet　　　Aluminium oxide　　　Silicon carbide

Abrasive materials

What we commonly call 'sandpaper' in school workshops actually consists of a range of different types of abrasive materials used for different wood-finishing situations. In the manufacturing process, a number of sharp irregular particles of man-made or natural grit are glued to a backing sheet of either paper or cloth. The grit sizes are graded and marked on the backing sheets as shown. Generally speaking, the lower the number, the coarser the grit size will be. Some abrasive materials are more efficient for resisting wear and clogging with wood dust than others and therefore are more expensive.

Sandpaper Selection Chart						
Paint Stripping		**Bare Surfaces**		**Between Coats**		
·COURSE· 60 ·COURSE·	·COURSE· 80 ·COURSE·	·MEDIUM· 100 ·MEDIUM·	·MEDIUM· 150 ·MEDIUM·	·FINE· 180 ·FINE·	·FINE· 240 ·FINE·	·FINE· 320 ·FINE·
heavy stripping	moderate stripping	surface leveling	surface smoothing	between coats surface smoothing	surface smoothing with a finer finish	final finish

use grit

Crushed glass

This is a relatively inexpensive type of abrasive, commonly called glasspaper. Glasspaper is used mainly on softwood to prepare for a paint finish.

Garnet

Garnet paper is formed from natural crushed garnet, which is relatively sharp and hard-wearing. The advantage of garnet is that the sharp edges break off during finishing and form fresh cutting edges.

Aluminium oxide

This abrasive is now commonly produced for sanding by hand and with power tools. It has the ability to resist clogging and is used especially for sanding dense hardwoods to a fine finish.

Silicon carbide

This is the hardest and most expensive woodworking abrasive. It is excellent for sanding hardwoods, MDF and chipboard, but it is most often used for rubbing down surfaces between coats of varnish and paint. Water is used as a lubricant, and the common name for this abrasive is 'wet-and-dry paper'.

Surface preparation

The cabinet scraper

If the surface to be finished has rough or rotary grain, it is better to start with a cabinet scraper. This is commonly a thin rectangular piece of spring steel, and its edges are burred over to give an even scraping edge. An alternative tool is supplied with a handle for a more comfortable grip when finishing a wood surface.

Sanding blocks

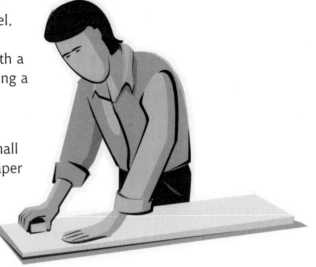

The standard method of sanding is to wrap a small cutting of sandpaper round the face of a sandpaper block and to grip both sides with fingers and thumb. The most common type of sandpaper block is made of cork or hard rubber, but some sanding blocks are shaped to take a standard strip of abrasive.

Sanding flat surfaces

The orbital power sander can be used on large surfaces; but sanding by hand, although it takes longer, is often the best method for finishing narrower components. It is better to sand all parts before assembly, especially inside surfaces that will be difficult to sand when assembled. Stand beside the bench so that you can rub the material along the grain with long smooth strokes. Work steadily and do not be tempted to rub across the grain, as this will leave scratches.

Raising the grain

When you have managed to attain a smooth finish on the surface, the grain will rise up when varnish is applied, and the surface will appear rough again. To prevent this from happening, wet the surface slightly with water and leave to dry. The grain will rise and can be sanded smooth again and filled with grain-filler.

Sanding narrow edges and chamfers

One of the most common faults seen in finished projects is corners, chamfers and edges that have been rounded over by over-enthusiastic sanding. Try to keep away from edges when sanding so that they remain crisp and clean.

Quick Test

1. Why is silicon carbide the best-quality abrasive?

2. Explain the term 'raising the grain'.

3. What is the purpose of 'raising the grain'?

Answers 1. Silicon carbide is the hardest and most expensive abrasive for wood, MDF and chipboard. It is also used in its finest form for rubbing down between coats as wet-and-dry paper. **2.** By wetting the grain, it rises up – this is called 'raising the grain'. **3.** A raised grain can be either sanded or scraped off to produce a smoother surface.

Application of finish

Sealing the grain

After finishing the surface of the wood satisfactorily, the grain is very often porous and an application of varnish would sink in rapidly, so it has to be filled with a suitable grain-filler which is either transparent or the same colour as the wood. Before applying grain-filler, make sure the surface is completely free from blemishes and dust. Apply the paste with a cloth or pad, rubbing the material well into the grain using circular strokes, and then leave to dry after cleaning off the excess with a clean cloth. Sanding sealer, in liquid form, is applied to finer wood grains with a brush and acts in the same way as grain-filler, and may require an additional coat after drying and rubbing down.

Top Tip
Good grain-filler can be made by mixing fine sawdust from the same wood with PVA glue to a smooth paste.

Top Tip
Internal curves can be effectively sanded using a piece of sandpaper wrapped round a piece of dowel of suitable size.

Types of surface finish

Oil stains

Sometimes called solvent stains, these are the most commonly used stains, made from oil-soluble dyes, and are thinned using white spirit. Oil stains are easy to apply evenly, will not raise the grain, and dry quickly.

Spirit stains

Traditional spirit stains are made by dissolving dyes in methylated spirit. Their main disadvantage is that they dry very quickly, which makes even application difficult and can leave darker patches of overlapping colour.

Top Tip
It is always best to seal the wood surface with sanding sealer before applying varnish.

Water stains

Water stains are supplied as a ready-made stain or in the form of powder that can be dissolved in hot water. Their main advantage is that they dry very slowly, and an even coat can easily be applied. They are now very popular in teaching workshops, but have a tendency to raise the grain and leave a rough surface, so it is essential to wet the wood and sand down prior to applying water stains (see p. 109, 'Surface preparation').

Acrylic stains

Acrylic stains are a new generation of wood stains that raise the grain less and are more resistant to fading. Acrylic stains tend to darken the wood and may have to be diluted in the appropriate solvent before application.

Wax polishes

There are two types of wax polishes: those that go straight on to bare wood, and those applied on top of sealed surfaces. You must read the manufacturer's instructions carefully to ascertain which type of wax polish you are using. Apply the wax polish sparingly with a soft cloth and leave for about thirty minutes before buffing with a clean soft cloth. Hard wax, such as carnauba, is used for producing a fine friction polish on turnery.

Sanding sealer and wax-polish finish

Sand the surface in the appropriate stages, clean off the dust, apply a coat of sanding sealer and, when dry, rub gently with fine steel wool or silicon carbide paper. Apply a second coat of sanding sealer and repeat the process. When you judge the surface to be completely sealed, apply wax, polish as described above. The surface may require about four to five coats of wax, but this can make a simple though effective surface finish.

Top Tip
The basic rules of wood-finishing are: polish, rub down, clean.

Quick Test

1. Why is it important to read the manufacturer's instructions before applying a surface coating?

Answer 1 So that the appropriate type of polish can be used, the right number of coats can be applied, and the drying time of the material determined.

Types of surface finish (cont.)

Oil finishes

Oiling wood is so easy that success is practically guaranteed, provided you have prepared the surface adequately and you don't leave the oil to become sticky. Traditional linseed oil is excellent for both feeding the wood and producing a lasting finish. Its main disadvantage is that it takes up to three days to dry. There are a number of proprietary oils available now which are both non-toxic and quick-drying.

Oiling bare wood

Apply the first coat of oil to the wood surface with a soft brush, ensuring that all surfaces are thoroughly wet. Leave the oil to soak in for about fifteen minutes, then wipe off any excess with a soft cloth pad to ensure an even coating. After leaving for about six hours, use an abrasive nylon pad to rub the oil into the wood in the general direction of the grain. After leaving for about another six hours, apply a third coat in the same way. Leave the last coat to dry thoroughly, and burnish with a duster to produce a soft sheen.

Varnishes and lacquers

Varnishes are effectively clear paints. They offer very good protection to the surface of the wood without obscuring its grain. Water-based varnishes, which are often described as acrylic varnishes, tend to look milky and leave the surface with a slightly cloudy appearance after drying. However, the main advantages of water-based varnishes are that they offer good protection and are very quick-drying, non-flammable and, importantly in a school environment, safe to use. Lacquers are similar to varnishes, producing a decorative high-gloss finish. Many lacquers are now developed to produce a hard, quick-drying finish.

Preparing to varnish

Wear disposable gloves and protect all surfaces, give yourself space in which to work, and organise your system of coating each surface in turn. Use a good-quality brush with a full head of bristles, making sure that it is clean. Small flecks of dust or dried varnish in the brush will tend to loosen while you work and ruin the job. Immediately after use, secure the lid firmly on the tin and clean the brush in the proper solvent.

Quick Test

1. What are the most important points to observe when applying varnish?

Answer 1. Listen to or read the instructions. **2.** Use a clean brush. **3.** Do not overload the brush. **4.** Avoid runs and drips. **5** Apply thin even coats. **6.** Allow drying time. **7.** Rub down between coats. **8.** Clean the brush thoroughly after use, and store away properly.

Applying varnish

The main skill in applying varnish is its even distribution over the surface, without causing runs and drips. Load the brush and strike off the excess on the inside edge of the tin so that it doesn't run down the outside. Paint the varnish evenly onto the surface, first with the grain and then across it to spread the finish evenly. It pays to have the workpiece set out on protection sheets with everything to hand. When finishing a carcase, it is best to first think how to coat the surfaces without getting varnish on your hands and clothes. If the inside of the carcase is to be finished first, do this first, along with the back edges. Then place the box upside down on thin sticks and apply a coating of varnish to the sides and front. The workpiece can now be left in place to dry.

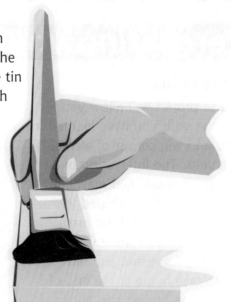

Paint finishes

A great many types of paints are produced for application to household furniture and for external use.

- Water-based paints have the advantage of being water-soluble and so can be easily thinned down for application; also, stains can be quickly removed. The disadvantage of water-based paints is that they can only be used for internal work.

- Oil-based paints come in a wide variety of colours, providing both gloss and matt finishes. Some types of oil-based paints are quick-drying. Oil-based paints can be thinned with white spirit for applying a number of coatings.

- Acrylic-based paint is produced with a number of modern additives in order to provide applications to suit a number of situations and for both internal and external use.

Paint primer and knotting

- Primer is a thin matt coating applied to new wood to form a slightly rough base in preparation for the application of paint.

- Knotting is an application used mainly on softwoods to prevent knots from coming loose and to prepare the surface for paint or varnish.

Top Tip
Paint should not be applied to projects until the grade has been externally verified – joints may be covered, and you may not get the most credit for your good work.

Quick Test

1. Name one advantage and one disadvantage of using water-based paint.

2. Why is it important not to overload the brush when applying paint or varnish?

3. Why is it important to raise the wood grain when preparing a surface for finishing?

Answers 1. Water-based paints can be thinned and stains removed easily, but can only be used for interior applications. **2.** To prevent drips and runs on the finished surface. **3.** So that it can be sanded off before the application of the paint or varnish. If the grain is not raised and sanded, it may rise up through the finished coating and cause roughness.

Course Project

Intergrating your learning

Further skills

The course project will allow you to develop the skills you have learned in the units and will consist of elements of these units. The integration of a flat frame, a carcase, and machining-and-finishing work is included in this final piece of work, and the project is designed so that you will enjoy each stage of the progression and have an artefact to take home at the end of the course. The project also allows you a further opportunity to improve on skills learned in the units.

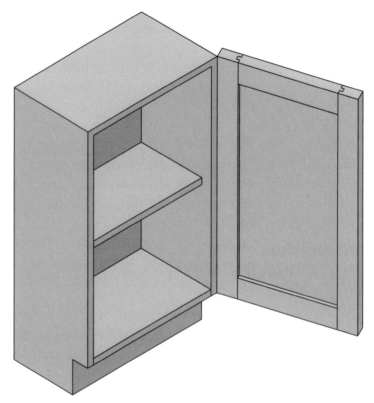

How your skills will be assessed

As with the previous units in the course, you will be assessed continually on various aspects of the work, such as: the degree of difficulty of the practical tasks; the quality of the finished project; the accuracy achieved in assembling the parts; the range of tools and equipment used; how you plan the stages of the work; and how well you observe the setting-up and operation of machines and general safe working practices.

Degree of independence

The degree of independence you demonstrate when working is one of the most important aspects of the assessment – but that doesn't mean that you shouldn't ask for help or direction when required.

Quality of the course project

The main criteria for assessing the final project will be: the tightness of the joints; how closely you worked to the tolerances and sizes described in the working drawing; the quality of turnery; the quality of other machining processes; and the quality of the surface finishing.

Range of tools and equipment

You will be assessed on your ability to identify the parts of the range of tools and equipment you have used so far. You will also be marked on any malfunctions and their remedies, the demonstration of set-up checks and safe working practices.

Course projects and skills

Wall cabinet

A wall cabinet consists of a carcase with shelves and a turned door handle.

Jointing skills and processes

The main carcase is constructed using stopped housing joints to fit the top, bottom and middle shelves and the ends are shaped top and bottom. The back is rebated into the sides and is shaped at the top. A turned spindle is fitted into drilled stop holes in the sides at the bottom with a slot for removal. The door is framed using haunched mortice-and-tenon, or corner halving joints, and a ply or mirror panel is rebated or grooved in.

Storage stool

This stool consists of a box carcase for the storage unit and a framed panel fixed to each side-forming the legs.

Jointing skills and processes

The leg frame is formed in one single long flat frame incorporating through haunched mortice and tenons in broad rails at each end and stub mortice-and-tenon joints near the centre for the bottom rails. The frame is then divided to form the side leg frames with hand grips cut in the broad top rails. A turned spindle forms a cross-rail between the bottom side rails.

Granddaughter clock

This is a fairly advanced project consisting of essentially three carcases. The top carcase forms the housing for the clock face and is reflected in the bottom carcase, which forms a stabilising feature of the design.

Jointing skills and processes

The long slender mid-carcase houses the pendulum. All three carcases have rebated corners and back panels. Front panels are formed using flat frames that are either key-mitred at the corners or formed with haunched mortice-and-tenon joints. Hand-run or pre-machined mouldings are fixed and mitred round the horizontal edges of the top and bottom carcases. Dead ply panels are rebated into the top and bottom carcases, and glass or clear plastic is fitted to the centre door. Matching knob handles are fitted to the top and middle doors.

Top Tip
Don't try to be too independent at the risk of making mistakes. Ask if you are not sure, and work steadily.

Quick Test

1. Explain the main aspects of quality you will be assessed on in the course project.

Course project – clock

Sequence of operations

Jointing skills and processes

This project consists of a carcase structure which houses the clock pendulum, and a divided flat frame with haunched mortice and tenons at the corners and stub mortice and tenons at the mid-rail. The face and top detail consists of a shaped crown piece with turned finial and chamfered capping pieces. The clock face is rebated into the top half of the frame, and the back is rebated into the rear.

The working drawing

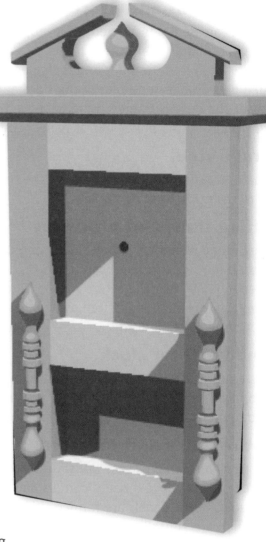

You should examine the working drawing closely to establish how you are going to tackle the project. The way in which you do this depends upon a number of things such as how far on you are in the course, or when you can get access to machinery. For example, you may have to start with the turnery so that the group can get maximum use of the turning lathes. In any case, you should become familiar with every aspect of the working drawing, the sizes of the various parts, and the kinds of joints you are going to use. For the purposes of this guide, the sequence of operations follows the progression of the units of the course, but a start can be made with any part of the project so long as the processes are planned beforehand. The stages of work should include checking material sizes, setting out, joint-cutting, assembly and finishing.

The cutting list

The object of producing a cutting list, as has been indicated before, is to assemble all the material sizes on a grid in a standard recognisable form so that the wood can be cut and machined to these sizes by a workshop technician. As part of Intermediate coursework, you will be presented with a partially completed cutting list, and, by studying the sizes on the drawing, you should be able to complete the task.

Making a marking-out rod

A marking-out rod can be made from a thin strip of ply or white flat painted hardboard, so long as you can scribe clear and distinct lines across the surface. Accurately transfer the length of the flat frame on to the rod, and square these lines across. Mark on the length of the horns, about 30–50 mm outside of the length-lines. Transfer the frame breadth and measure off from the length-line, and square across.

Top Tip
It is better to mark clearly what each line represents on the rod and to indicate by arrows.

Planning the operation

When you receive the material for the flat frame, it may be all in one length, so your first task is to check the sizes against the cutting list and the working drawing. Work out the overall length of the stiles, including horns, and cut two to length. In the case of the clock frame, there are three rails, which should now be cut to the size between the shoulders plus two stub-tenon lengths.

The sequence of marking out

The next stage is to ensure that all edges are square and that breadths are slightly oversize to allow for cleaning off. Scribe a face side and face-edge mark on each part. So that all shoulders are exactly in line, it is better to pair the stiles, mark on the sizes, and square across the face edges while they are clamped together in the vice. The best, and most accurate, way to transfer sizes on to the material is to place the edge of the rod along the material length and mark on all sizes including horns and haunches.

Marking out the joints

With reference to page 39, gauge on the mortice-and-tenon joints in sequence from the face side, and mark all haunches on the face edge.

With reference to pages 34 and 35, gauge on the half lap joints in the same way.

Forming the joints

After all waste wood is carefully marked, tenons should be cut as described, paying particular attention to the haunch detail. The corner halving joints are formed in the same way.

Morticing

After conducting the safety checks, the material is set up in the machine with the face edge upwards and the face side flat against the fence. The morticing operation should proceed as described.

Top Tip
A good habit to get into is to pair sets of stiles and rails with the face edge up and face sides together.

Top Tip
Always gauge from the face side so that, if the gauge setting is not exactly central, the parts of each joint will still match.

Top Tip
Always set the frame parts in the machine in the same way, face side to the fence, so that if there were mistakes in gauging the mortices will be cut correctly.

Top Tip
When morticing the haunches, stop before the measured depth and hand-chisel when fitting each joint.

Quick Test

1. List the main sequence of operations in building a flat frame.

Answers 1 Check material sizes. 2. Pair stiles and rails. 3. Mark out joints. Cut joints and fit joints. 5. Glue and assemble frame. 6. Flush off and prepare surfaces.

The clock (cont.)

The carcase

The sides and ends of the carcase are drawn in by direct measurement or by using the marking-out rod, as described on page 71 (making a carcase).

Setting out

As with a flat frame, it is very important when marking out a box carcase construction that the sides, ends and partitions are held together and matched so that, when marks are squared round each part, the shoulders and housings are exactly in line. It is a good idea to make the depth of the rebated butt joints at the corners the same as the width of the panel rebates, i.e. half the material thickness.

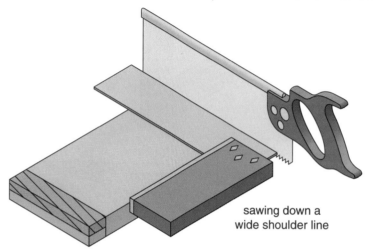

sawing down a
wide shoulder line

Cutting the joints

With reference to pages 71 and 72, cut the rebated corners and hand-run the edge rebates as described. An additional rebate can be run on the bottom end of the carcase to house the back panel more securely. All rebates should be smooth, even and square. Pay particular attention to squaring shoulders without over-sawing and thus weakening the tongue, which should be flat and even.

Assembling the carcase

When gluing and clamping a carcase (see pp. 58–9):

- ensure that all the inside faces have been cleaned and sanded;
- ensure that the joints are all tight when glued and clamped;
- check that all the rebates are lined up to receive the back and front panels;
- square the carcase with the try square;
- remove all surplus glue.

Top Tip
When clamping a carcase, remember to fit clamps top and bottom to ensure even pressure across all the corner joints.

Fitting the back and front panels

Fitting the clock-face panel

Plane the two reference edges of the ply panel square to each other, then fit into the top and side of the rebate, and mark with an X as shown. Fit the panel into the corner, and mark off the side edge. After fitting the top half, the bottom is open, but this edge should be planed smooth and square. Glue and pin the panel in place.

Fitting the back panel

The procedure for fitting the back panel is the same; but ensure that there are no rough edges showing on the outside of the panel.

Quick Test

1. List the main sequence of operations in building the carcase.

Fitting flat frame to carcase

Sequence of operations

Step 1

Check flushing of all the outside surfaces of the **carcase** to within tolerances. Sand carefully.

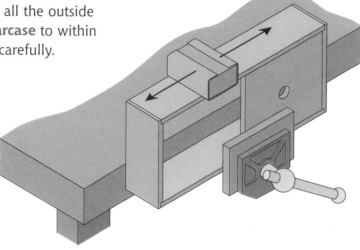

Step 2

Ensure that the front face of the carcase is true.

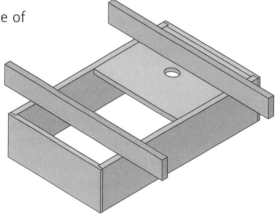

Step 3

After planing any raised edges to true flatness, rub the carcase on a large sanding board to render it perfectly true.

Top Tip
Check for wind (or twist) using two straight edges, as shown in the diagram alongside.

Step 4

Ensure that the back surface of the flat frame is true by flushing off any lipping, avoiding any taper to the outside edges. Sand carefully.

Step 5

Place the carcase on the flat frame in the correct position (check the margins all round), and ensure that there are no seams showing round the edges between the two meeting surfaces. Make sure that the clock-face panel is fitted tightly to the back face of the flat frame.

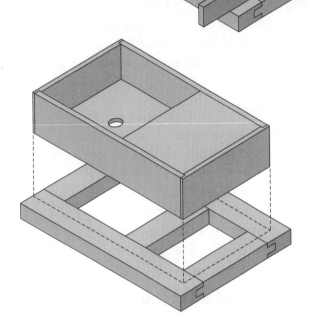

Step 6

Apply glue evenly round the meeting edges of the carcase, and fit to the flat frame. Apply **clamps** with protection blocks, as shown.

Top Tip
Wipe off all surplus glue immediately with a wet paper towel to avoid staining.

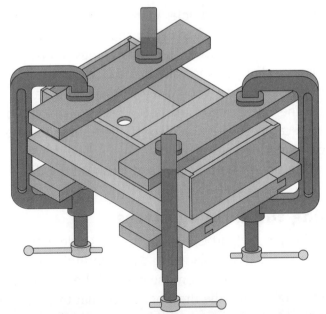

Quick Test

1. Explain the sequence of fitting the flat frame to the carcase.

Answers **1. Make sure that the surfaces of the carcase and the flat frame that meet are absolutely flat. 2. Place the carcase on the flat frame with all the margins even. 3. Set the clamps in position, and apply even pressure.**

Forming and fitting the top detail

The top facing plate

Part A is prepared by choosing and then marking the best face side and face edge for the front and top. Sand one end square on the disc sander and, after measuring the length and squaring across, sand to within the tolerance. Next, set the marking gauge to the size of the chamfer, and gauge the front edge and ends, working from the top surface and edges. Setting the workpiece in the vice, plane down evenly at an angle to the gauge-lines. Fit the workpiece vertically in the vice, and plane the ends in the same way, except that you must use a slicing action with the plane on the end grain, working slightly upwards.

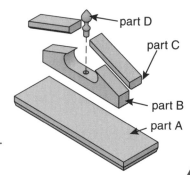

part D
part C
part B
part A

The crown piece

First, cut and finish the crown piece to length on the disc sander. The best face side should be to the front. The face edge is fitted to part A and must be square and true. Mark out the centres of two holes to form the curve, and transfer the angle with a sliding bevel from the drawing. Connect the circles and angled lines to form tangents to the curves, as shown.

Top Tip
Do not plane across the grain unless a same-size block is held against the work, as shown.

Forming the curved shaping on the crown piece

Carefully drill out the two holes with the Forstner bit in the drilling machine, set to depth and with a piece of scrap fitted underneath to form clean holes. With the workpiece clamped vertically in the vice, cut the remainder of the waste wood away with a coping saw, cutting to the waste side of the line. Finish the shaping by means of a cabinet file and a piece of medium sandpaper wrapped around a piece of 25-mm dowel. Saw down to the waste side of both bevels, and finish on the disc sander.

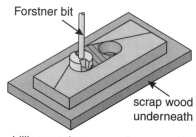

Forstner bit

scrap wood underneath

drilling out the crown piece – part B

Forming the capping pieces

The capping pieces (part C) are cut from a single length of material that is first checked and planed to width and thickness. Gauge and form a 5-mm chamfer on one edge of the material. After lifting the angles from the drawing, check that these angles will form vertical faces at the top and bottom of both pieces when fitted to the crown piece. Ensuring that the chamfer is to the front bottom edge, mark on the lengths and angles, and cut to the waste side of each line. After finishing the angled faces smooth and flat on the disc sander or sanding board, carefully glue and pin each capping piece in place, taking care with their alignment.

Top Tip
When finishing the bottom straight surface between the two curves, make sure that there are no bumps or dips where the bottom edge meets the curve.

Forming the split turnery

Both the split turnery and the finial piece (part D) may be turned from a single turnery blank (see pages 94 and 95). The outline shape of the split turnery and the finial should first be drawn on paper to an appropriate design. The shapes may then be transferred to a ply template so that you can gauge your progression towards the finished shape when turning on the lathe. The turning of the work can proceed with frequent testing, using the template, as the shape is formed. When forming the finial, it is best to produce a peg tail of say 8 mm in diameter and 60 mm in length for fixing to the top detail.

ply template

> **Top Tip**
> To attain a perfect alignment, pin each part with a single pin at its end, and then straighten through with a rule or straight edge.

Finishing the turnery

Before the turnery is parted off and split, it can be finished with sandpaper while being turned on the lathe. This can be done by lightly holding a strip of sandpaper at both ends under the turnery and gently sanding each curve and corner (see finishing on the lathe, page 99). Varnish can be applied in the same way with the machine at a slower speed or friction-polished with carnauba wax.

> **Top Tip**
> Remember, you will be assessed on the accuracy of two or three main dimensions that you have established on the profile.

Parting off and splitting the turnery

When the polish is quite hard, the turnery can be parted off using the appropriate lathe tool. The ends can be finished carefully by hand with sandpaper and polish. The technician or your teacher will now split the main turnery feature on the band-saw using a parting jig. The sawn faces of each half can be sanded perfectly flat on a sanding board,

Final assembly of the top detail

The final assembly of the top detail can be carried out as follows:

- find the centre of the top plate (part A) by drawing in the diagonals, and drill through the centre with a twist drill the same diameter as the tail peg on the finial;
- after finding the centre of the bottom edge of the crown piece (part B), drill with the same drill;
- next, fix the top facing plate (part A) in position on the top of the clock carcase by gluing and carefully clamping;
- when the glue is set, drill partway through the top plate into the clock, and fit and glue the assembly in position by means of the finial peg;
- ensure that all surplus glue is wiped off immediately, and check the alignment of the parts.

Completion of detail and final finish

Any prepared clock face can now be fitted along with the clock mechanism and pendulum. Ensure that the pendulum leg is cut to an appropriate length if necessary. All surfaces should now be given a final sanding with 180-size grit sandpaper. Take care to remove all pencil marks, scratches and other blemishes at this stage.

Quick Test

1. Explain the sequence of operations in producing the split turnery and finial.

Answers 1. Draw out the desired shape of the split turnery and finial. **2.** Produce a template for gauging turnery shapes. **3.** Prepare block for turning. **4.** Turn to template tolerances.

How to improve your grade – summary

Essential knowledge and understanding

Safety in the workshop
- Work safely and according to instructions at all times when using hand and machine tools.
- If you develop an awareness of the dangers to yourself and others without being afraid, you will become more confident and accomplished.
- Get to know the safety checks on machines before each operation.

Recognition of basic parts of common fixed machine tools
Recognition of basic parts of common power tools
Knowledge of hand tools and their parts
- Keep the bench tidy at all times, and work in a careful and methodical manner.
- Get to know the name of each hand tool, its parts and its different applications, and use hand tools and equipment correctly.
- Be aware of the condition of cutting tools and how to correct any faults including sharpening edges.

Knowledge of a range of common hardwoods and softwoods
Develop a working knowledge of a small number of hardwoods and softwoods, their characteristics, common uses and how to recognise them.

Knowledge of a range of man-made boards
Develop a working knowledge of a small number of manufactured boards, their characteristics, common uses and standard thicknesses.

Abrasives
Develop a knowledge of a small range of abrasives, grit sizes and their application to wood-finishing.

General knowledge
Learn the names, functions and qualities of a small number of the following:
- common fixed machine tools;
- common power tools;
- wood glues;
- wood finishes.

Skills visible on completed project

You should be aware of the parts of the project that will be visible on examination, such as the joint between the carcase and the flat frame, the exposed haunches of mortice-and-tenon joints, any internal curved work, chamfers and so on.

Flat-frame construction

Material preparation, and measuring and checking materials and sizes
- Develop accuracy when transferring sizes from a working drawing to the materials and setting out.

- Always pair rails and stiles.
- Carefully square and prepare the ends of materials.
- Interpret working drawings, and lift off sizes.
- Learn the process of selecting and scribing the face sides and face edges.
- Be systematic.
- Learn to arrange and set out the joints.
- Always gauge from the face side or the face edge.
- Take care in marking out a rod or template(s).
- Work to tolerances.
- Saw and finish to a curved pre-drawn line – check for squareness and blemishes.
- Saw across the grain to a shoulder-line – square the shoulders.
- Check and pair shoulder sizes – parallel stiles and rails.
- Overall sizes should be within tolerance.

Flat-frame joints

- Develop the process of setting out, cutting and fitting joints in a methodical manner.
- Develop a methodical system for setting out, cutting and fitting joints.
- Always gauge from the face side or face edge.
- Halving joints – ensure that all shoulders are square and clean, and that tenon faces are flat and smooth. Cut exactly to the gauge-line, and do not twist.
- All joint edges should be crisp and square.

Mortice-and-tenon/bridle joints

Whether morticing by hand or by machine, always stop just short of the end of the mortice and vertically chisel down to the line. Don't chisel beyond the end-line, and never lever the mortice chisel on the end of the mortice as these will leave telltale gaps. When hand-morticing, always keep the chisel absolutely vertical when chiselling, so that the mortice is true. When cutting tenons (and end halving joints), always saw down the tenon in three stages before cutting the shoulder, as described, and pare off any roughness down to the gauge lines. Over-sawing the shoulder will weaken the tenon. Take great care not to produce a tenon with a twist, as this will affect the alignment of the frame when assembled. When cutting a haunch, make sure you don't mortice too deep or pare down the sides of the tenon haunch too much. Take great care when fitting the haunch – any gaps will show on the frame end when the horn is removed.

Assembling the flat frame and the carcase

When marking out joints, always lay out alternate rails or ends and stiles or ends with the face side up and the face edge towards you, as described. Remember to number corresponding adjacent joint parts where the numbers won't be cleaned off. Always dry the frame first so that any trimming-off and adjustments can be made before gluing. Apply clamps evenly, don't over-tighten to close a shoulder gap, and try running a saw-kerf down the opposite shoulder. Always square the frame and remove surplus glue immediately, as this will otherwise leave a mark which will show through any varnish finish. Check for twisting. If a slight twist is found, leave the workpiece weighted down on a flat surface until the glue is set.

Flat-frame joints (cont.)

Cleaning off a flat frame
Care should be taken with this process so that the frame finishes within the tolerances. Particular care is required at the outside edges of the face, as any tapering will show clearly from the frame end.

Carcase joints

Rebated butt joint
When cutting a rebated butt joint, take care to create a straight and square shoulder. Do not over-saw when cutting shoulders, as this weakens the joint and is visible in the finished work. When finishing to the end gauge-line, make sure the rebate is finished straight and square, since any irregularities will show as gaps.

Through and stopped housing joints
All shoulders should be straight, even and cut inside the lines to form a tight joint. Care should be taken, when fitting shelves, not to plane too much off and not to leave gaps at the exposed front edge. In a stopped housing, make sure that there are no gaps caused by making the front notch too deep.

Grooving and rebating
Make sure that the groove or rebate fits the panel thickness, and run a smooth and even cut with no rough edges that will show. When rebating, always keep the rebate plane square and tightly held into the edge, so that the cut is square and even.

Fitting the flat frame to the carcase
In the case of the clock, both the meeting faces should be carefully planed and sanded so that there are absolutely no gaps showing around the edges.

Curves and tapers
Taper planing to a pre-drawn line in the clock detail. The angles should be matched and squared across without twist to receive the capping pieces. The quality of a chamfer depends on how crisp and even the chamfer is throughout its length and on the return along the ends. There should be no rounding caused by over-sanding. Great care should be taken in finishing the internal curves of the crown upstand and in forming a straight and smooth edge between these two curves.

Check the quality and the alignment of turnery
Make sure that both the split turnery and the finial are produced to the required tolerances in terms of both diameter and length. This is normally achieved by producing a shaped profile as accurately as possible to the template or to a shape you have previously made. Split turnery should be flattened on a sanding board before gluing to ensure a close fit. The pieces should also be exactly square across from each other.